THIS BOOK BELONGS TO:

____

EGMONT

We bring stories to life

First published in Great Britain in 2020, by Dean,
an imprint of Egmont Books UK Ltd
2 Minster Court, 10th floor, London EC3R 7BB

www.egmontbooks.co.uk

Written by Daniel Lipscombe
Edited by Craig Jelley
Designed by Ian Pollard
Illustrations by Matthew Burgess
Cover designed by John Stuckey and Ryan Marsh

This book is an original creation by Egmont Books UK Ltd.

ISBN 978 1 4052 9702 8

70884/004
Printed in Italy

ONLINE SAFETY FOR YOUNGER FANS

Spending time online is great fun! Here are a few simple rules to help younger fans stay safe and keep the internet a great place to spend time.

- Never give out your real name – don't use it as your username.
- Never give out any of your personal details.
- Never tell anybody which school you go to or how old you are.
- Never tell anybody your password, except a parent or guardian.
- Be aware that you must be 13 or over to create an account on many sites. Always check the site policy and ask a parent or guardian for permission before registering.
- Always tell a parent or guardian if something is worrying you.

Stay safe online. Any website addresses listed in this book are correct at the time of going to print. However, Egmont is not responsible for content hosted by third parties. Please be aware that online content can be subject to change and websites can contain content that is unsuitable for children. We advise that all children are supervised when using the internet.

100% UNOFFICIAL

ROBLOX ANNUAL 2021

CONTENTS

HELLO READERS

Hello and welcome to the wonderful world of Roblox!

Whether you're a new player or have been roaming the world's biggest games platform for ages, there's always something fun to find. Roblox has millions of great games and worlds to explore. We love diving into somewhere new and finding exciting jobs and pets for players to enjoy.

In Roblox, you can truly be anything you want – why not be a baker? Or run a little shop? Perhaps you want to race around cities delivering pizza or capturing bad guys? Maybe you just want to find some cool games to play with friends, or try your hand at an obstacle course?

Whatever you choose, there's something for you here. If it's your first time truly jumping into Roblox, we're here to help and guide you to some of the best games. If you're more experienced, then we've set you some challenges. No matter why you're reading this book or playing Roblox, we're all here to have fun.

So, settle down at your PC, or grab your controller or smart device, load up Roblox, choose a game to play and remember to stay safe. Above all, have fun!

THE WORLDS OF ROBLOX

So much happens in Roblox, we've struggled to cram the past year's events into two pages – it's overflowing with new experiences! We can't forget what your fellow Robloxians achieved and which games they played the most.

100 MILLION MONTHLY PLAYERS

Perhaps the biggest news of recent months, Roblox hit 100 million monthly players! That's a lot of people playing games. Not only that, but those millions managed to play over 1 billion hours of games together.

DEV STARS

Roblox has become one of the most popular places to create games. Anyone young or old, no matter the level of experience, can create what they want. Not only that, but they can encourage other players to try out their creations. Some creators have gone on to program other games or even pay for their education thanks to the Roblox games they made.

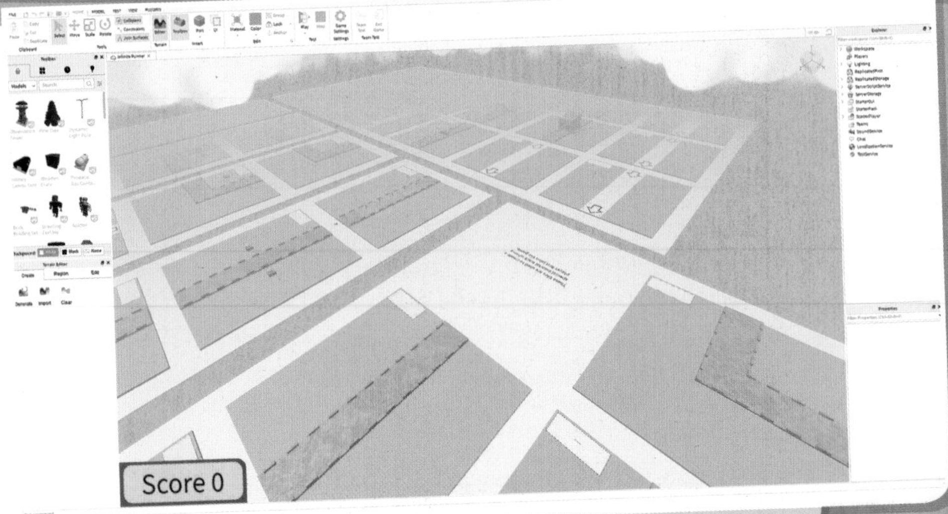

SUMMER CREATOR CHALLENGE

Players around the world were encouraged to create their own games and worlds with the help of Roblox. Creators were given tools and a pre-built program that taught users how to build games slowly and with guidance. Roblox helps teach people how to code and encourages players to explore their creativity.

EDUCATION

Teachers were able to use Roblox to build lessons for their students. Not only was this used to teach coding, but also any number of ideas from educators in other subjects. Teachers and students together could create places to try out new ideas!

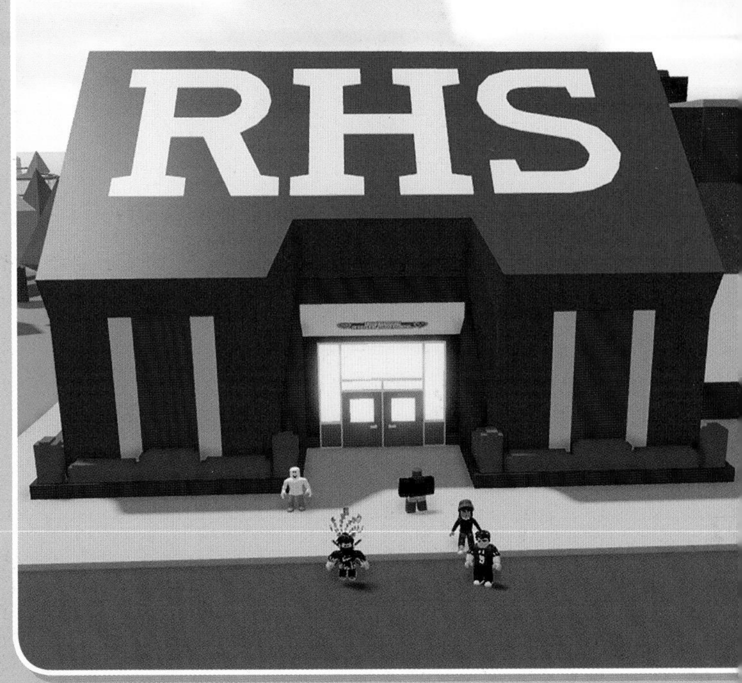

MENTAL HEALTH AND CYBER SAFETY

Together with parents, teachers and doctors, Roblox worked hard to make the game safer than ever for players of all ages. By creating new safety settings, it became easier for players to enjoy their favourite games. Roblox aims to cut down on bullying and harassment. Players have access to tools that can instantly remove danger or trouble, through blocking and reporting offending players.

ALL-TIME TOP 10 VISITS

There are so many games to play in Roblox. But which ones have been visited the most?

1. MeepCity
2. Adopt Me!
3. Jailbreak
4. Royale High
5. Murder Mystery 2
6. Work at a Pizza Place
7. Welcome to Bloxburg
8. Prison Life
9. Flee the Facility
10. Super Hero Tycoon

PLATFORMS AND CONTROLS

Roblox fans can now play their favourite games wherever they go, but switching from one device to another might be a little bit confusing. Here's a handy guide to show how to play Roblox on PC/Mac, Xbox One and on mobile.

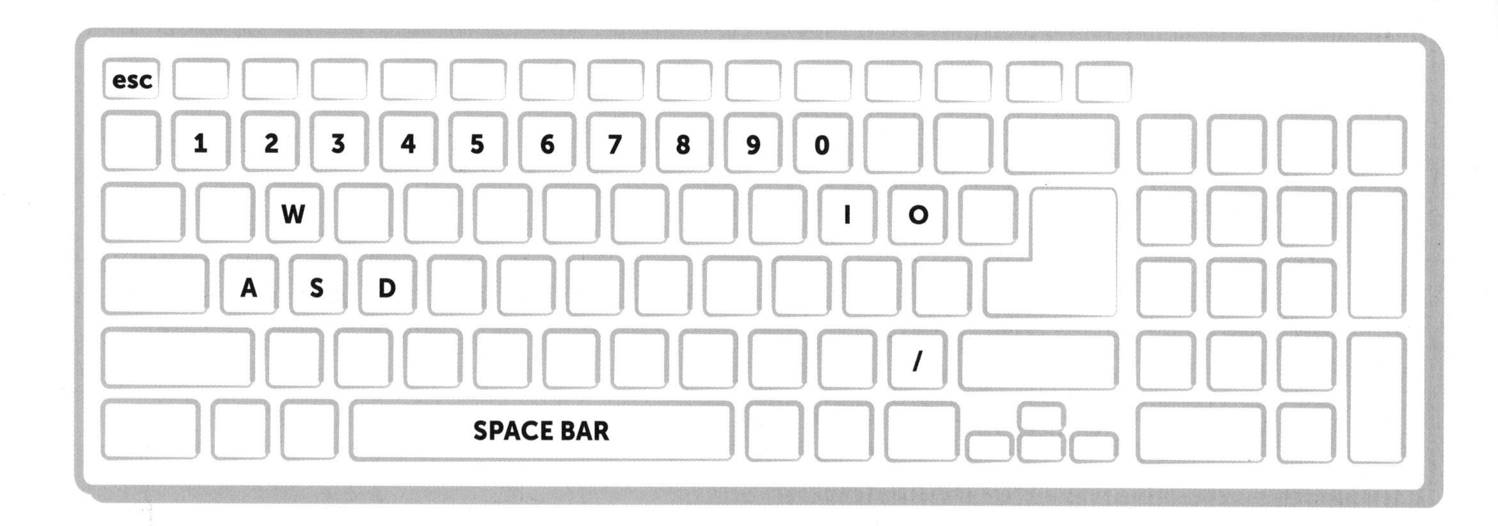

KEYBOARD

- [WASD] – Movement
- [Space bar] – Jump
- [Number Keys] – Equip/unequip Items
- [I/O] – Zoom in/out
- [/] – Chat
- [Esc] – Menu

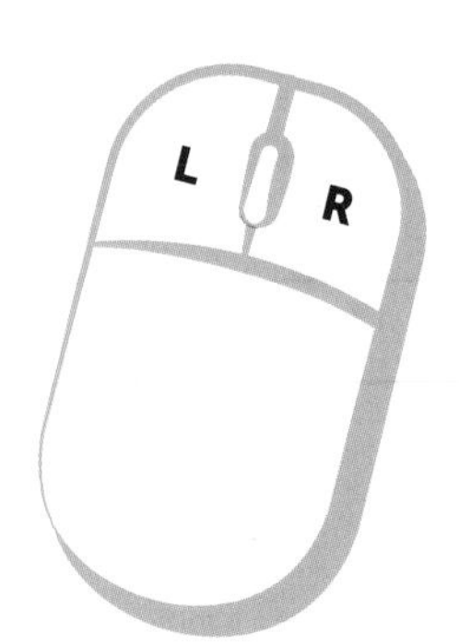

MOUSE

- [Left Click] – Use equipped item
- [Right Click] – Rotate camera

WHICH PLATFORM IS BEST FOR ME?

There's no easy answer to that question, but here are some things to consider. Mobile and computer users have access to a larger library of games than on the Xbox version of Roblox. But some people just love to play games with a controller. The obvious advantage to mobile devices is that you can take your gaming on the go!

MOBILE DEVICE

Most of the mobile controls are quite simply completed by tapping the screen. To select and equip items or navigate menus, you'll just need to tap the relevant on-screen button. However, there are a couple of overlay controls to note too:

- [Virtual Joystick] – Movement
- [Jump Button] – Jump

XBOX

- [Left Stick] – Movement
- [A] – Jump
- [B] – Back/cancel
- [LB/RB] – Cycle through equipped items
- [RT] – Use item
- [Right Stick] – Rotate camera
- [Right Stick Press] – Zoom in/out
- [Menu Button] – Roblox menu

5 ACTION GAMES

Roblox can be a cool place to chill out with friends, but sometimes you need that high-octane, fast-paced gaming to pass the time in a flash. Try these five excellent action encounters to get the adrenaline flowing.

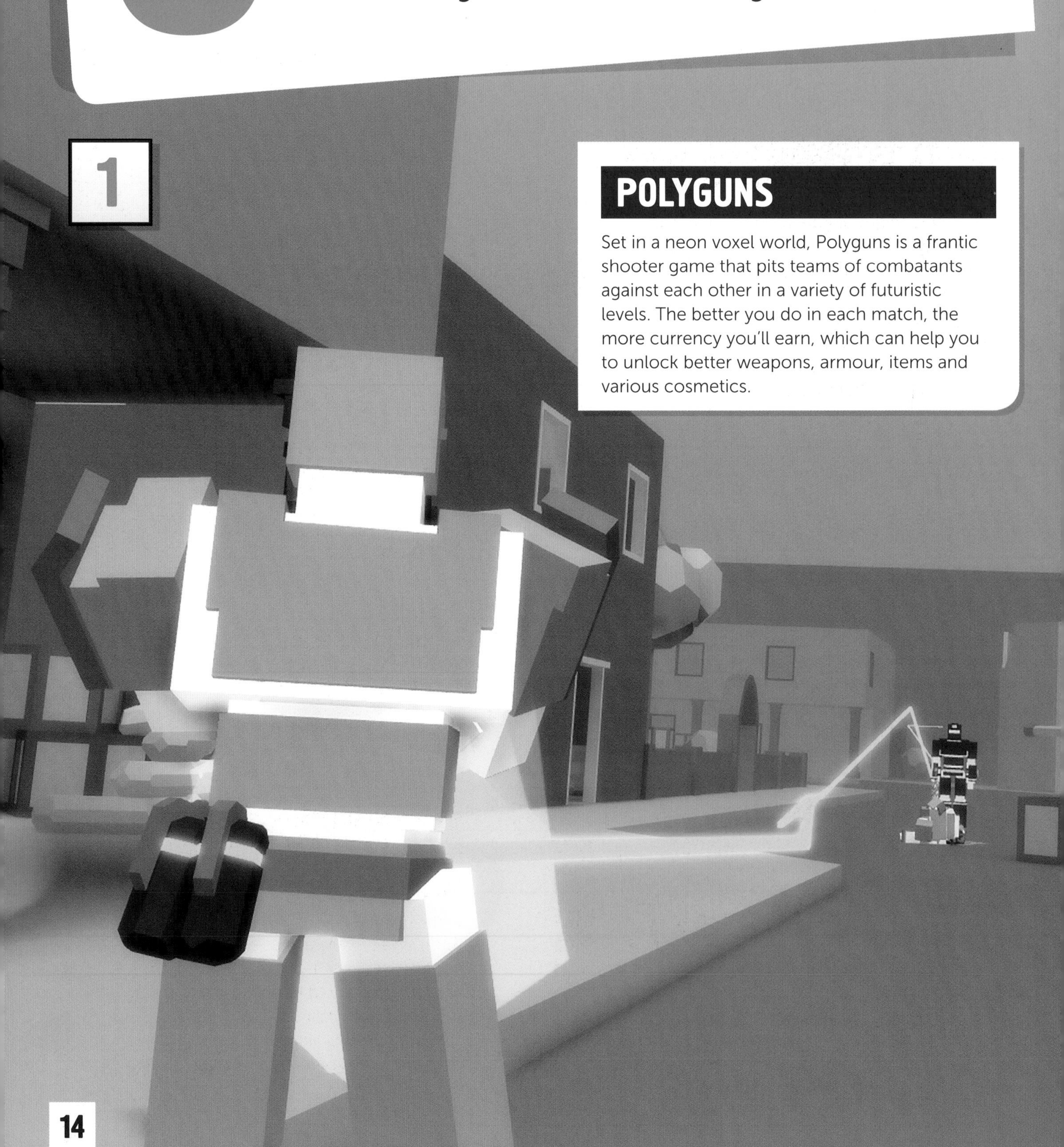

1 POLYGUNS

Set in a neon voxel world, Polyguns is a frantic shooter game that pits teams of combatants against each other in a variety of futuristic levels. The better you do in each match, the more currency you'll earn, which can help you to unlock better weapons, armour, items and various cosmetics.

2

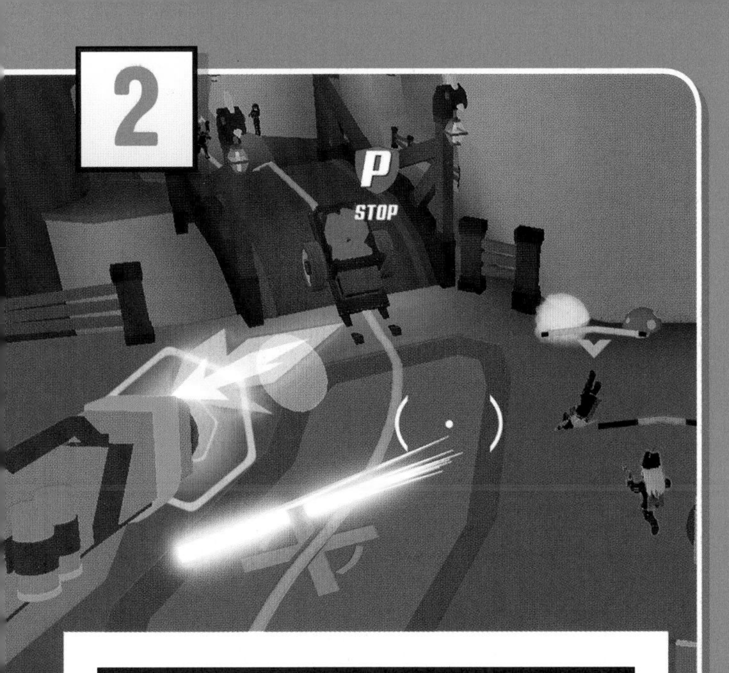

Q-CLASH

Pick one of eight unique heroes, each with their own skills and abilities, and take to the battlefield in Q-Clash. This amazing hero shooter tasks teams with a number of objectives, like capturing points on a map, or pushing a cart from one side of the map to the other! The frantic action really pushes the boundaries of what's possible on Roblox.

3

ADVENTURE UP!

You can hunt for treasure, upgrade your gear and learn amazing spells in Adventure Up! but the real fun begins when you visit the dungeons, which are crawling with gigantic monsters for you to battle!

4

WORLD // ZERO

Enter this brightly coloured world as one of three classes: swordmaster, mage or defender. Each of them has powerful abilities that you can use to take down bad guys and as you progress, you'll be able to specialise your character down a certain path to unlock even cooler skills!

5

APOCALYPSE RISING 2

Sequel to the original survival sim on Roblox, Apocalypse Rising 2 is one of the most loved action games on the platform. You have a wide, open world to explore, but you're not alone. Terrors are lurking around every corner, from shuffling zombies to other lethal players. Do all you can to survive.

STARTING POINTS

If you're new to Roblox, the number of games to choose from can be daunting and it can all feel a bit of unfamiliar. We've picked some games that will throw you in the middle of some awesome experiences and help you learn the ropes.

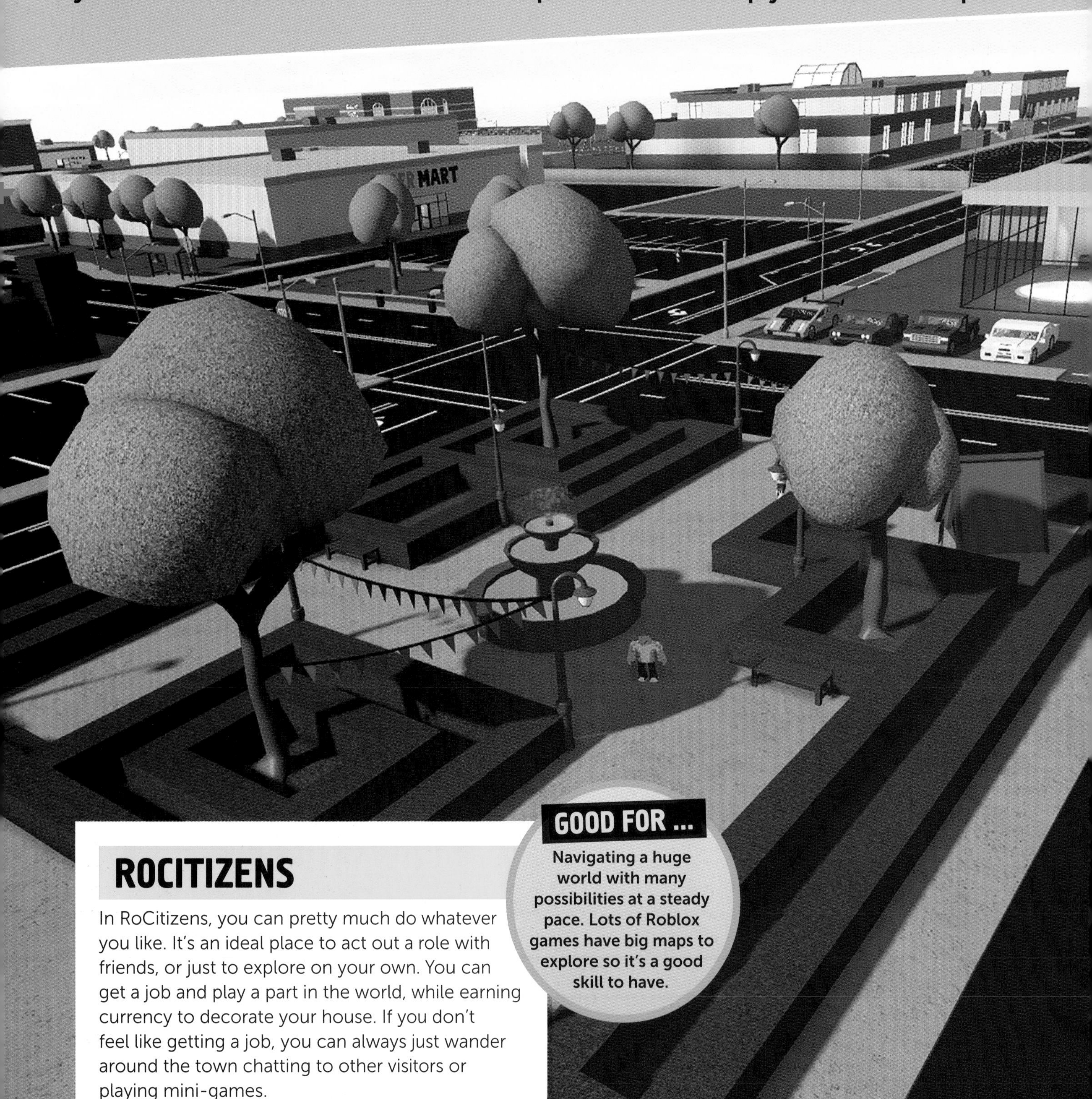

ROCITIZENS

In RoCitizens, you can pretty much do whatever you like. It's an ideal place to act out a role with friends, or just to explore on your own. You can get a job and play a part in the world, while earning currency to decorate your house. If you don't feel like getting a job, you can always just wander around the town chatting to other visitors or playing mini-games.

GOOD FOR ...

Navigating a huge world with many possibilities at a steady pace. Lots of Roblox games have big maps to explore so it's a good skill to have.

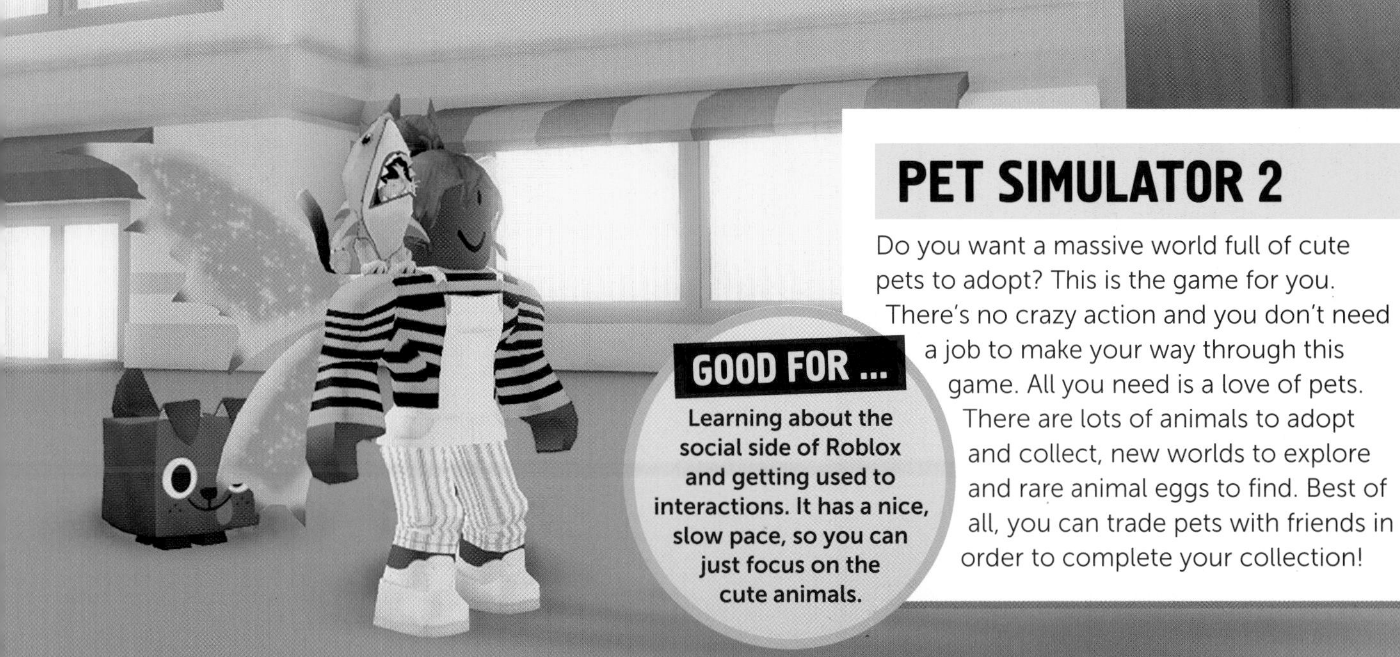

PET SIMULATOR 2

Do you want a massive world full of cute pets to adopt? This is the game for you. There's no crazy action and you don't need a job to make your way through this game. All you need is a love of pets. There are lots of animals to adopt and collect, new worlds to explore and rare animal eggs to find. Best of all, you can trade pets with friends in order to complete your collection!

GOOD FOR ...

Learning about the social side of Roblox and getting used to interactions. It has a nice, slow pace, so you can just focus on the cute animals.

WORK AT A PIZZA PLACE

In this game you can take one of three different jobs in the world of making pizzas. If you want to make the pizzas, you'll spend time in the kitchen preparing, cooking and boxing the pizzas ready for the customers. You could work the counter if you prefer, talking to customers and serving them with fresh food. Lastly, you can deliver the pizzas with super-fast bikes or cars.

GOOD FOR ...

Getting used to the controls and look of Roblox. Trying different jobs gives you a greater range of experience.

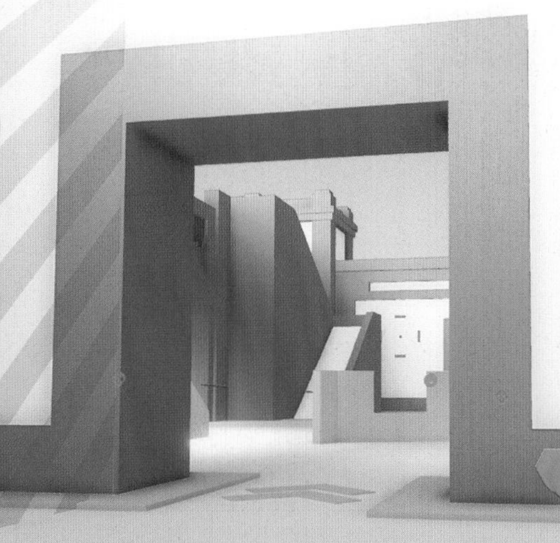

GOOD FOR ...

Working on controlling your avatar quickly and reacting to other players. It will be tricky at first, but you'll soon master the skills needed for lots of games.

BIG PAINTBALL

For players who want some fast and crazy action, Big Paintball is a great way to find it. Lots of players are competing for crazy kill streaks and trying to take out their friends by splattering them with paint. There are lots of challenges and ways to level up your character, so you can either drop in for the odd game or play a lot to unlock more fun ways to play.

BEST VEHICLES

Do you like to go fast? Perhaps you dream of racing cars down long stretches of motorway, or drifting supercars around sharp corners? Well Roblox is the place to fulfil that dream! Some of these cars have a more urgent need for speed than others that just look really cool. Here are some of the best we've found across the many games of Roblox.

EDISON ROADSTER 2.0

ROBLOX VEHICLE SIMULATOR

Easily the fastest car in any of the Roblox games, the Edison Roadster looks sleek and is tuned for raw power. It's not cheap. In the Roblox Vehicle Simulator it will cost you $12,000,000, but you'll leave everyone in your rear-view mirror. Described in game as 'The petrol killer', this car will smash all speed records and you'll look cool doing it. The maximum speed of this beast is over 400mph, so strap in and get ready to feel the g-force!

ROCKET CARS

CAR CRUSHERS 2

Yeah, we kind of cheated with this one, seeing as any car in Car Crushers 2 can become a rocket car. Grab your favourite 4-wheel vehicle, strap a rocket to the back and blast your way around the map, launching yourself into the air. Plus, in Car Crushers 2 the aim is to trash the cars as much as you can. So use that rocket to your advantage and smash up the car until it's about to explode, then throw it in the car blender! Rockets make everything better!

VOLT BIKE

JAILBREAK!

The Volt Bike looks like it jumped straight out of a futuristic arcade game and onto the streets of Jailbreak! Its gorgeous glowing paintwork does make it a bit harder to hide from the cops, but they'll have trouble catching up to you as it's one of the fastest vehicles in the game! It only seats one, so you'll have to leave your fellow escapees behind – they'll forgive you when you're speeding into the sunset.

HELICOPTER

MADCITY

Helicopters are just cool. There are no two ways about it. They're fast, noisy and nimble. Flying through the air in one of these awesome machines takes some practice, but looks as cool as anything. You'll be the envy of lowly car-drivers all over MadCity. There's a reason they always appear in TV shows and films, they rule!

A BOAT

BUILD A BOAT FOR TREASURE

Okay, so we're cheating again, but not without good reason. Boats are great. Boats you build yourself are even better. In Build a Boat for Treasure, you're tasked with doing just that; building an awesome boat to find some shiny treasure. You can create whatever you want, as long as it's seaworthy! And once you've built and launched it on to sea, you get to be a pirate on the search for riches!

CAREER QUIZ

There are dozens of different jobs you can role-play on Roblox. Can you work out just a handful of them by rearranging the scrambled words below? There's a clue for each to help you out!

KERAB

Up early to make some dough.

ANSWER

REMIN

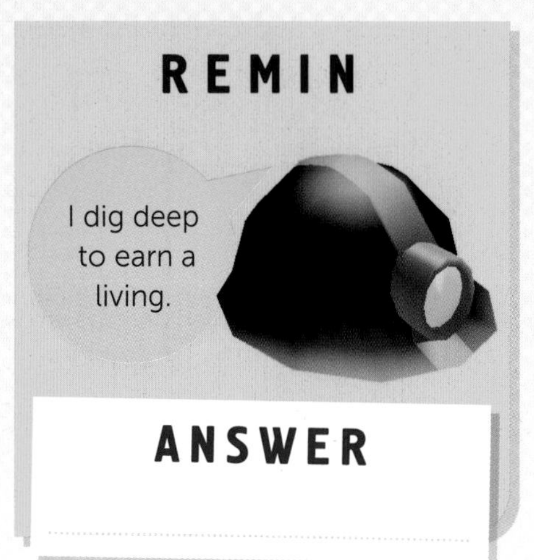

I dig deep to earn a living.

ANSWER

RETHCEA

It's time to learn!

ANSWER

TIREAW

Can I take your order?

ANSWER

TSIART

Beautiful creations are my job.

ANSWER

REPEKEPSHO

That will be £9.99, please.

ANSWER

CERAR

I hope I get first place.

ANSWER

TRODOC

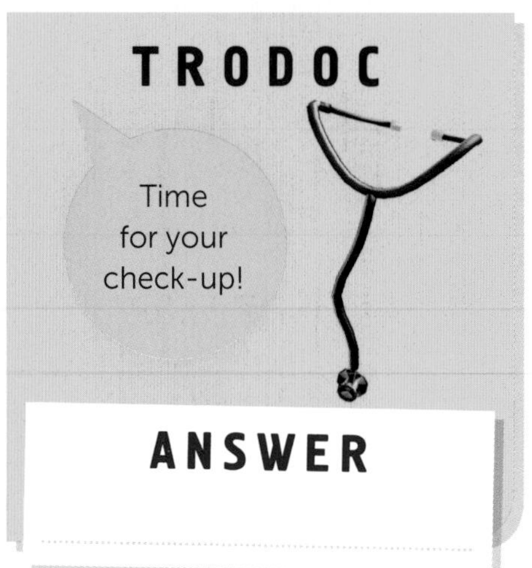

Time for your check-up!

ANSWER

RENKAB

I keep your money safe.

ANSWER

 Answers on page 69

YOUR FAVOURITES

There are a lot of games to keep track of in Roblox so this handy fill-out guide will help you keep a record of your favourite things along the way. You don't have to fill them all out at once!

FAVOURITE GAME

....

FAVOURITE JOB

....

FAVOURITE OBSTACLE COURSE

....

FAVOURITE VEHICLE

....

FAVOURITE PET

....

FAVOURITE DECORATING FURNITURE

....

FAVOURITE FRIEND

....

FAVOURITE FASHION ACCESSORY

....

FAVOURITE TYCOON GAME

....

FAVOURITE SHOP

....

5 ROLE-PLAYING GAMES

There are so many role-playing games to choose from and each of them offers something different. Whether you want to look after a pet, cook pizzas or hang around with friends in a virtual city, there's a game for you. Role-playing games are some of the best on Roblox!

ADOPT ME!

Perhaps you want to be a parent, or maybe you'd prefer to look after a puppy or a cute kitten. In either case, Adopt Me! is the game for you. You'll have a fully customisable house to make your own as you raise your family (or pet), hang out with friends, play in mini events and collect candy!

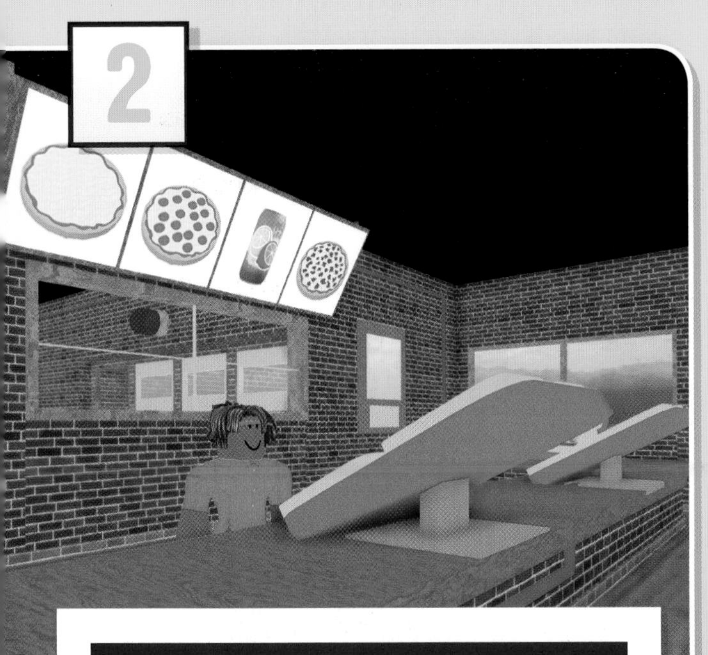

WORK AT A PIZZA PLACE

You can choose where you'll fit in best in the Builder Brothers Pizza team. If you love speeding around then you can deliver fresh pizza. Or maybe you want to make a tasty treat in the kitchen? Whichever you choose, you'll work with a friendly team to earn money and keep the town well-fed.

MEEPCITY

MeepCity is the place to be, and a place to be anything you want! Why not go to school and be the teacher instead of the student? Or race against your friends as a kart driver? Anything is possible! Don't forget about the cute little Meep pets you can take care of too!

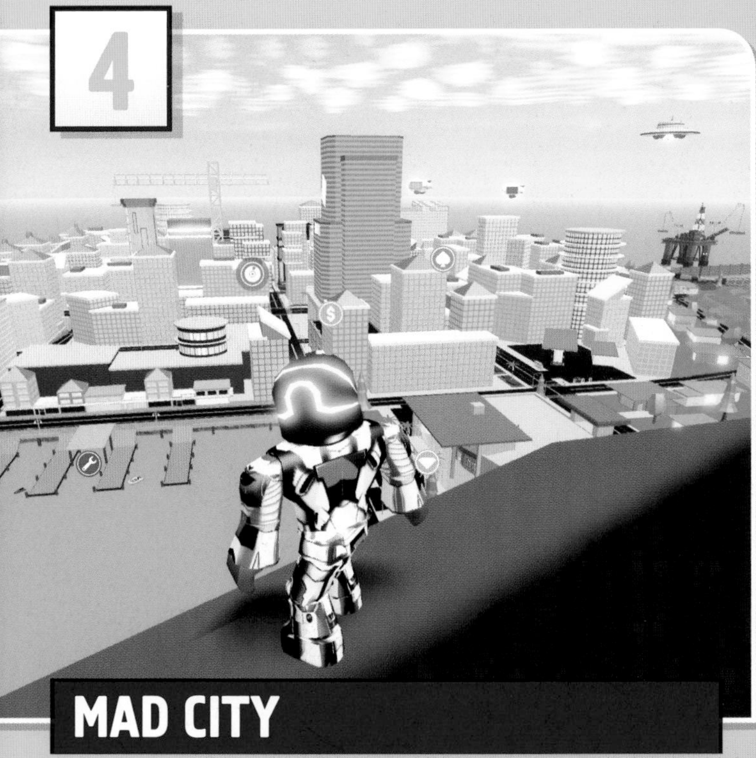

MAD CITY

In Mad City, it's up to you to decide whether you'll cause chaos or try to stop it. If you choose the path of light, you can be a superhero or cop, however, you may want to follow the path of darkness and play as a supervillain or criminal. If you've always wanted to be an action star, Mad City is the place to live out your wildest dreams!

WELCOME TO BLOXBURG

If you can imagine it, there's a strong chance you can do it in Bloxburg. Build huge houses, work in the shops or just wander around the massive world talking to people. There's always something to do and a role to play, whether you want to be a vet, doctor or delivery person.

SPOT THE DIFFERENCE

Can you spot the 10 differences between these two pictures?

 Answers on page 69

HIDDEN OBJECTS

Can you find the five objects below, hidden in this picture from Jailbreak.

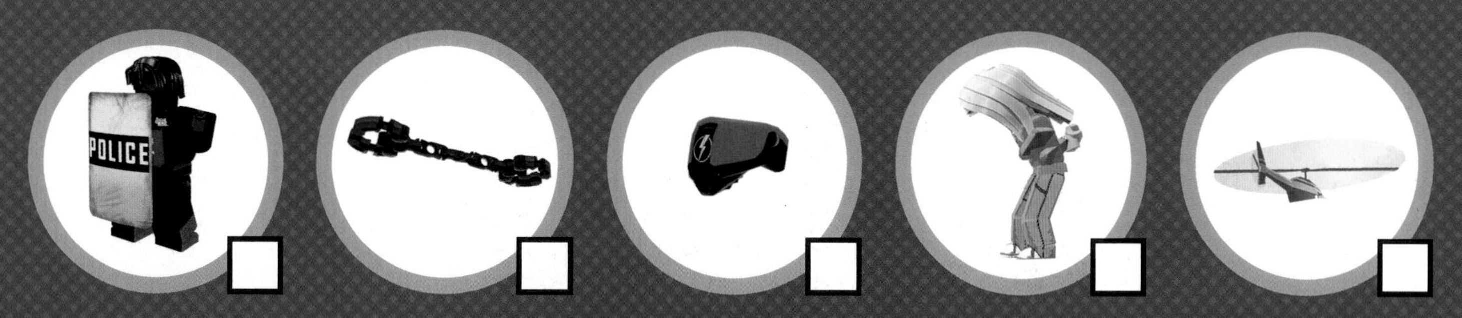

Answers on page 69

5 OBBY GAMES

Obby is a funny word. It's short for 'obstacle', meaning it's applicable to any game that features some sort of hazard-filled course. In order to get from start to finish you'll have to jump, crouch and slide to avoid danger.

1

MEGA FUN OBBY

This is the oldest obby on Roblox and with over 2000 stages, the BIGGEST too! The courses here range from easy to super-hard, but there are new courses added every few days, so if you get stuck you can come back to try a new one. With no theme running throughout, every course is a bit different.

Remember, you can change your controls if you're finding some of these games too difficult.

2

FLOOD ESCAPE

With five game modes and several difficulty levels, you and your friends will need to be fast if you want to beat the flood and reach the top of the monthly leaderboard. Great designs and courses really set apart this multiplayer racing obby.

3

ESCAPE THE DUNGEON OBBY

Nobody wants to be locked in a dungeon. The king has thrown you in the darkness for 100 years, but you know you can escape. Lots of obstacles stand in your way, however, so you'll need skill and speed to get out alive. The theme here is wonderfully creepy but ever so dangerous. Freedom is so close, thank goodness.

4

RAINBOW SLIDE OBBY

Not just a multicoloured obby, but also a hub for racing games. Slide your way to victory, or if you prefer, drive a car, steer a boat or ride a cart. As long as you avoid danger and reach the finish line, you can play however you like. Just remember to have fun along the way!

5

ESCAPE THE HOTEL!

Hotels are normally relaxing. Not this one. The manager has gone mad, trapping all the guests inside the building. You must escape, tackling over 20 courses, unlocking great items and accessories. Pack your suitcase, hand in your key and let's get out of here. Hopefully in one piece!

DESIGN YOUR OWN OBBY

A good obby can be fun on your own or to race against your friends. They sometimes require a lot of skill and often have a fun theme too. We've already looked at some of the best, so why not try creating your own? Use the key and example below to design your own obby!

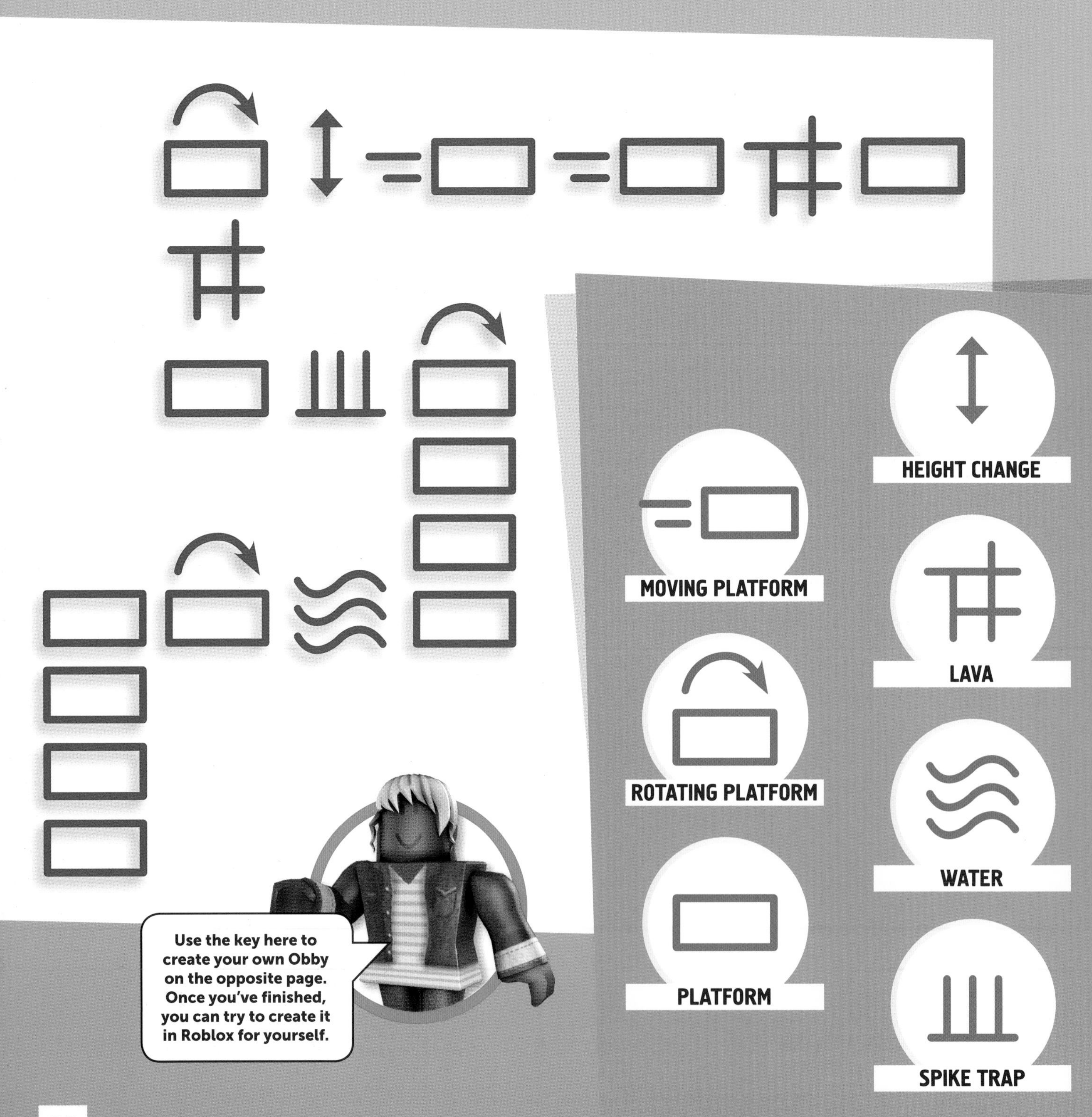

HEIGHT CHANGE
MOVING PLATFORM
LAVA
ROTATING PLATFORM
WATER
PLATFORM
SPIKE TRAP
Use the key here to create your own Obby on the opposite page. Once you've finished, you can try to create it in Roblox for yourself.

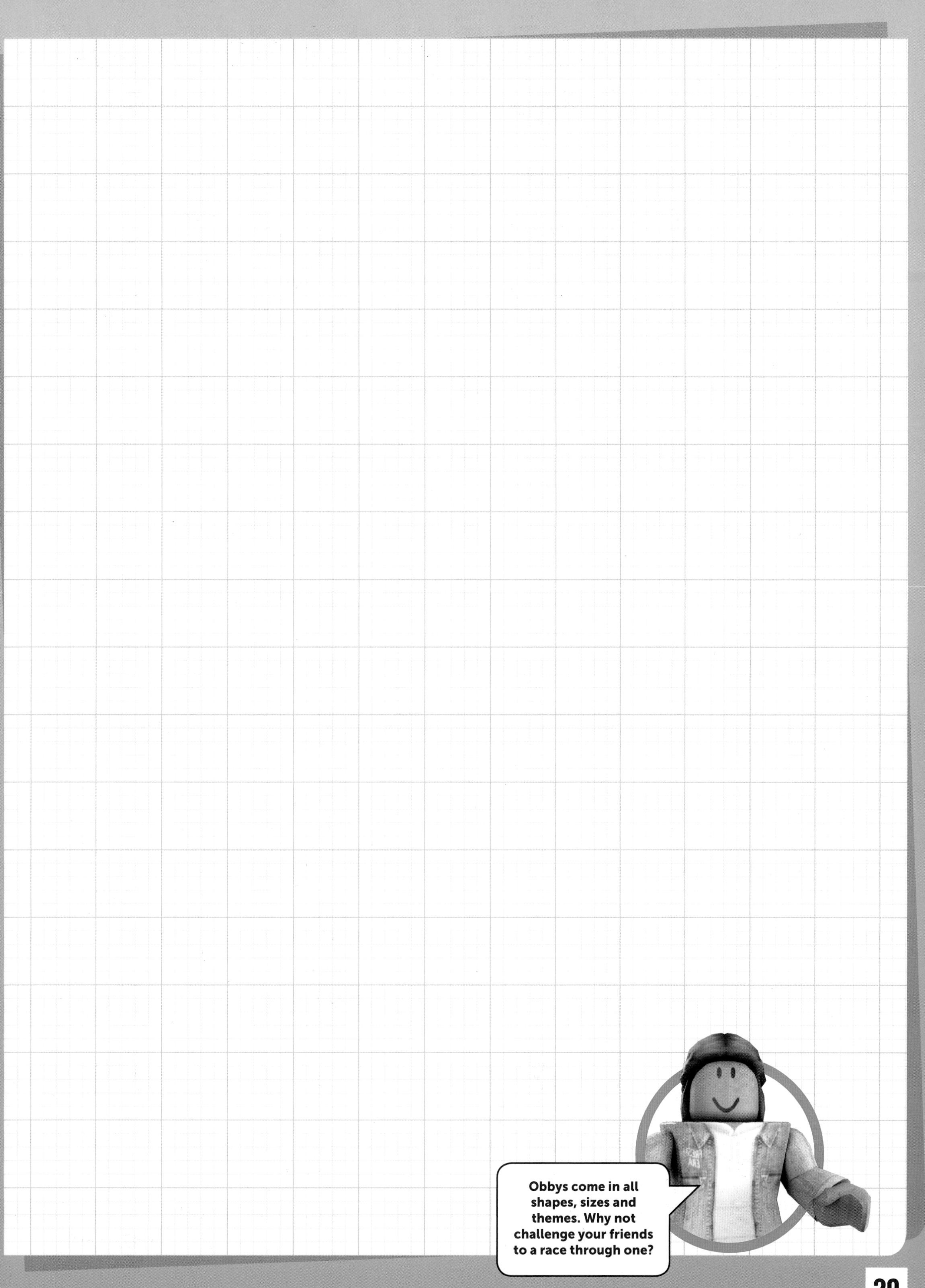
Obbys come in all shapes, sizes and themes. Why not challenge your friends to a race through one?

MAZE RACE

Obbys are all about dodging hazards and racing to the finish line. Do you think you can make it to the end of this fiendish maze without hitting any obstacles?

 Answers on page 69

FINISH

HIDDEN GEMS

There are thousands of games on Roblox and so many of them are amazing. It's very easy to stick to playing the most popular games on the homepage, meaning you might miss out on some wonderful experiences elsewhere. We've found some excellent games that might have escaped your attention.

HIDE AND SEEK EXTREME

We've all played Hide and Seek at one point, so you'll already know the basic rules; one player has to find their hiding friends. But this is extreme. What makes it extreme? Well, the seeker has some special tricks up their sleeve. For example, they can drop glue on the floor, meaning if a hider steps on it, they're frozen in place for a while, making them easier to find. This is a great game to play with mates!

SUPER BOMB SURVIVAL

In this explosive game, players spawn onto a map with one aim – to survive. However, bombs are raining down from the sky – some more damaging than others. As the game goes on, more bombs fall, walkways disappear and the last person standing is the winner. It's a nice short game filled with funny moments as players fly through the air or try to hide from harm. Thankfully, there are skills available to help you, but really the only way to win is to hope you don't get hit.

FASHION FAMOUS

Here's a game for those who love fashion or dressing up. At the beginning of each round, players are given a topic and must put together an outfit based on it. After dressing up, everyone votes on the outfits, with the most popular ones earning the most points. Play seriously or play wacky, Fashion Famous can be incredibly fun, especially if you have lots of friends playing. We love putting on as many silly accessories as possible to make people laugh!

TOWER OF HELL

So many obby games play horizontally across land. Tower of Hell requires players to head skyward, through a randomly generated series of obstacles. The catch here is you only have 8 minutes to reach the exit at the top. There are hundreds of dangerous obstacles to tackle over the different difficulty settings and the game only gets harder as the rounds go on – every time a player touches the door, it doubles the speed of the timer. Be fast or you won't get out at all!

VEHICLE SIMULATOR

For any players who love cars, this is the game to play! Here you can try out some of the world's most popular cars, and a few imaginary ones too. Race against others, test your speeds and raise money to buy even better cars. There's a lot to do away from racing too; you can upgrade your rides to make them fit your idea of style, plus you can head out and explore the area at your own pace, rather than break-neck speeds.

CAPTION THIS!

We love those moments of crazy action in Roblox, so we've taken pictures of some of our favourites. Can you write a hilarious caption to go with each one?

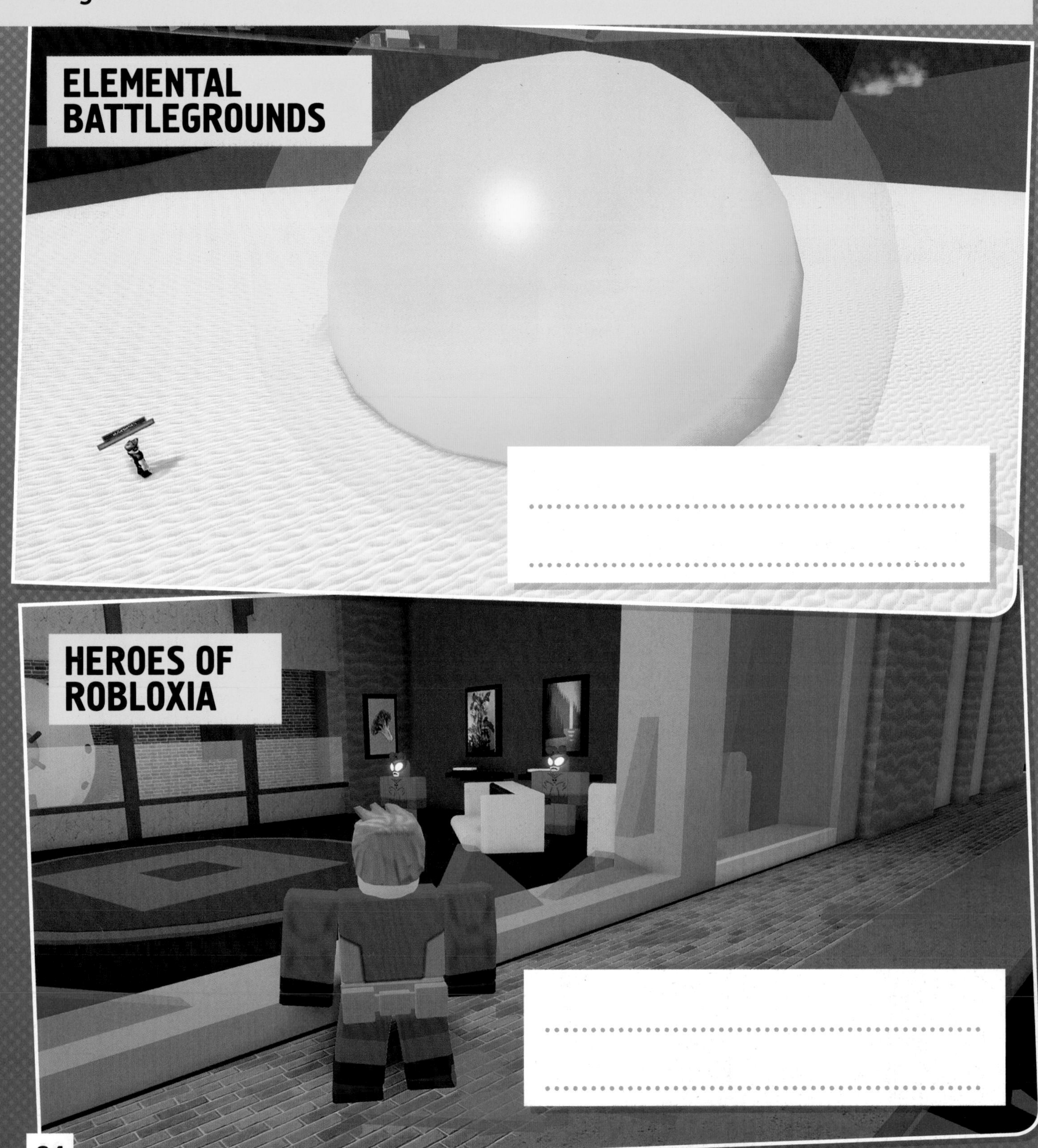

MADCITY

FANTASTIC FRONTIER

5 RACING GAMES

If you like to go fast, whether inside a sporty vehicle or not, then you'll want to speed through our list of the best racing games! They'll pit you against other rapid competitors or challenge you to beat your own best times.

1

SPEED RUN 4

Players keep returning to Speed Run 4 to try and improve their own times across 30 exciting obby courses. All they need to do is run and jump from one end of the level to the other as fast as they can. Of course, these aren't your average racetracks and require great skill as well as speed to navigate. A few new worlds were added in 2019 to give players a new challenge – you can even race across a moon!

DEATHRUN!

Deathrun! is one of the most successful racing games on Roblox, having appeared on the platform almost half a decade ago. It's another footrace against your fellow players, but this time, one of them is a 'killer' controlling traps and dangers along the course. The winner is whoever reaches the end and eliminates the killer first. There are plenty of different maps containing unique hazards that change the way you race too.

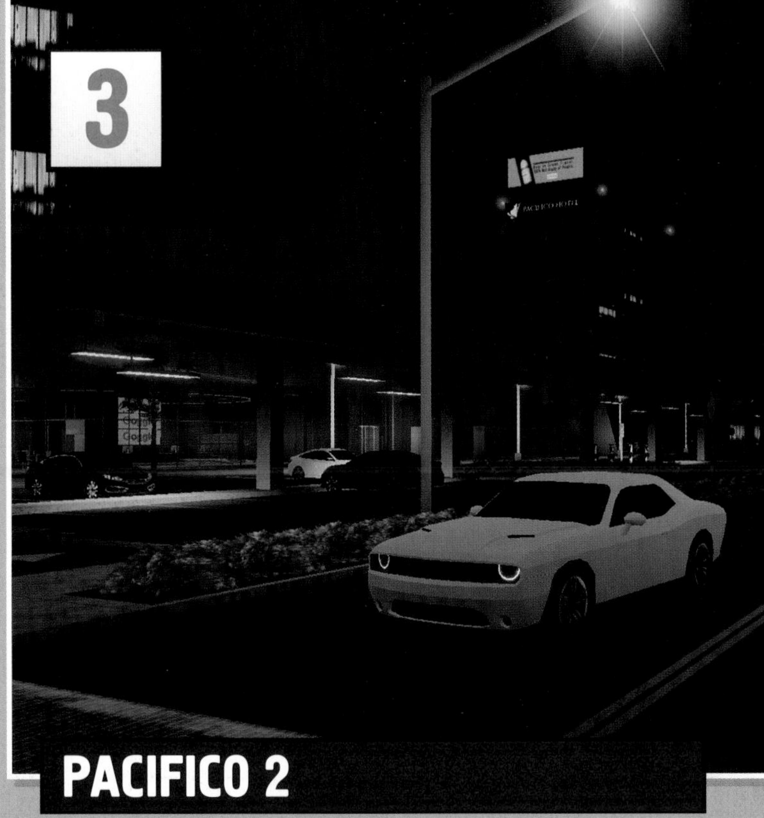

PACIFICO 2

Who needs a track? Pacifico is known for its vast array of cars, which were all individually designed for the game, and the world is as exquisitely crafted too. There aren't any set courses to race through, but you do have the freedom to challenge anyone, anywhere, in any vehicle. The only limit is your imagination!

ULTIMATE DRIVING: WESTOVER ISLANDS

There are several entries in the Ultimate Driving series, which are set in connected locations, and Westover Islands is easily the most popular. It's absolutely massive and gives you the freedom to pick your own vehicle and create your own fun. The best thing to do is become a police officer and chase down any cars that are breaking the speed limit. The game of cat and mouse that ensues is unpredictably fun and lets you put the pedal to the metal!

CAR CRUSHERS 2

When you've finally had enough of racing cars around, you can always have more fun smashing them to pieces. You can take to the destruction derby arena to duel with other cars until each vehicle is toast, or try one of the more interesting schemes like shredding them in a giant blender. Progressing through the game rewards you with tokens, which unlock new cars and accessories ... how do you feel about strapping a rocket to a sports car? Because that's where the fun begins!

CAR SUDOKU

Keeping cars in good condition means you need a lot of spare parts. Fill in the blank spaces so that there is only one of each car part in any row or column.

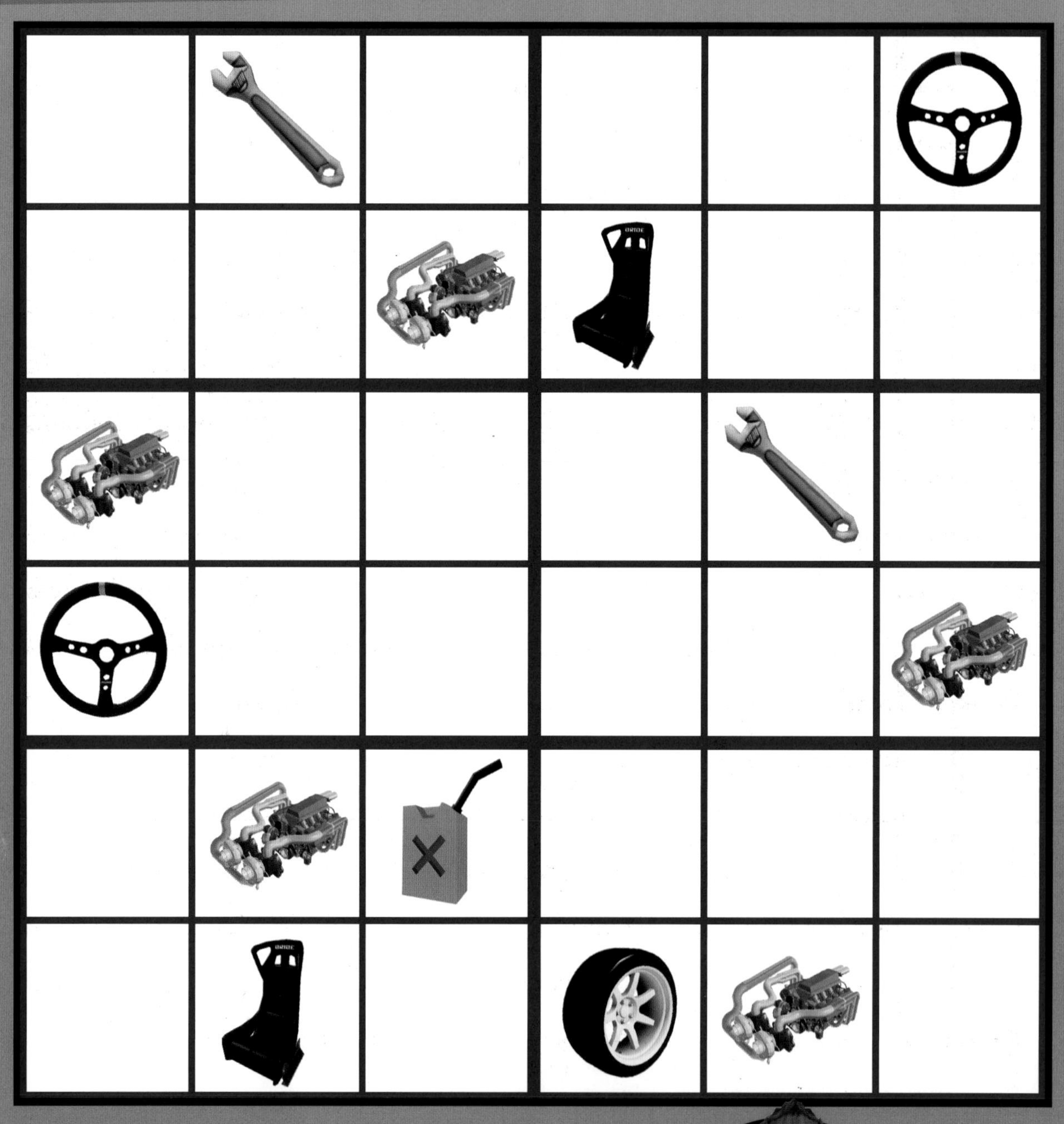

Which part of the car has the most fun? The WHEEEEEEEls!

Answers on page 69

SPEED
MAZE
Now it's time to burn rubber. Race your way through this tricky maze as fast you can. Will you be the first to make it to the flag?

Answers on page 69

10 OF THE BEST

So many games, so little time. Instead of searching endlessly through the Roblox game pages for something new to try, we've picked ten of the best games for you. Some have been played by millions, some by a fraction of that. But all of them show what can be achieved in Roblox!

1

ROBLOX HIGH SCHOOL 2

School can be lots of fun with the right friends and the right classes, which is why it's great that you can choose both in this game. If you don't want to go to art class, you can go shopping instead or even get a job. We, however, love the classes which act as mini-games and once we've finished for the day, we can hop in our sports car and head home for a spot of decorating!

NATURAL DISASTER SURVIVAL

One of the older games on the platform, Natural Disaster Survival requires players to stay alive through different disasters on one of the 16 maps available. With floods, sandstorms, fires and earthquakes to survive, you have to think quickly. Using items and tactics, you can experiment with different ways to stay alive. However, lots of fun can be had if you and your friends find yourself on top of a tower when lightning strikes!

MURDER MYSTERY 2

Do you want to be a detective and solve murder mysteries? Because that's exactly what you do here! Murder Mystery 2 was the first game to reach ten million visits and it's not surprising why. One person plays as the sheriff and it's their job to find the murderer with the help of innocent players who witnessed the crime. The best part is working together to solve the mystery and if the sheriff dies, another player can replace them.

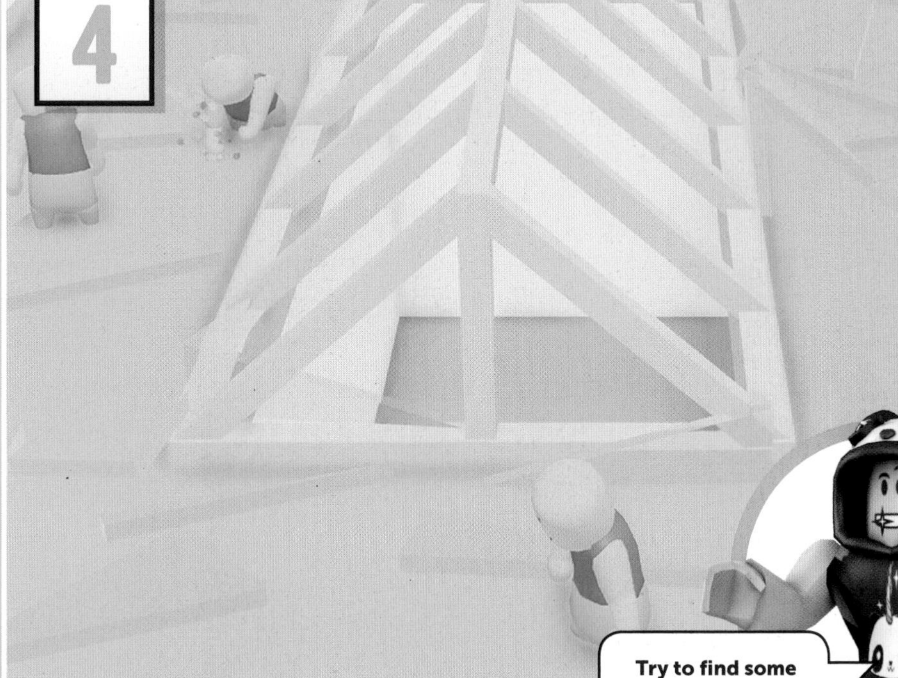

FLOPPY FIGHTERS

Press 'F' to fart. Now there's a special move we like! In this crazy fighting game, players have to hit each other to earn the most points. It sounds simple, but each fighter wobbles around on unsteady feet. It's great fun, especially in King of the Hill, where you need to stay on top of the hill to win ... but you keep sliding down. Coins activate things like anti-gravity or increase your size for even more fun.

Try to find some overhead cover to protect you from falling blocks!

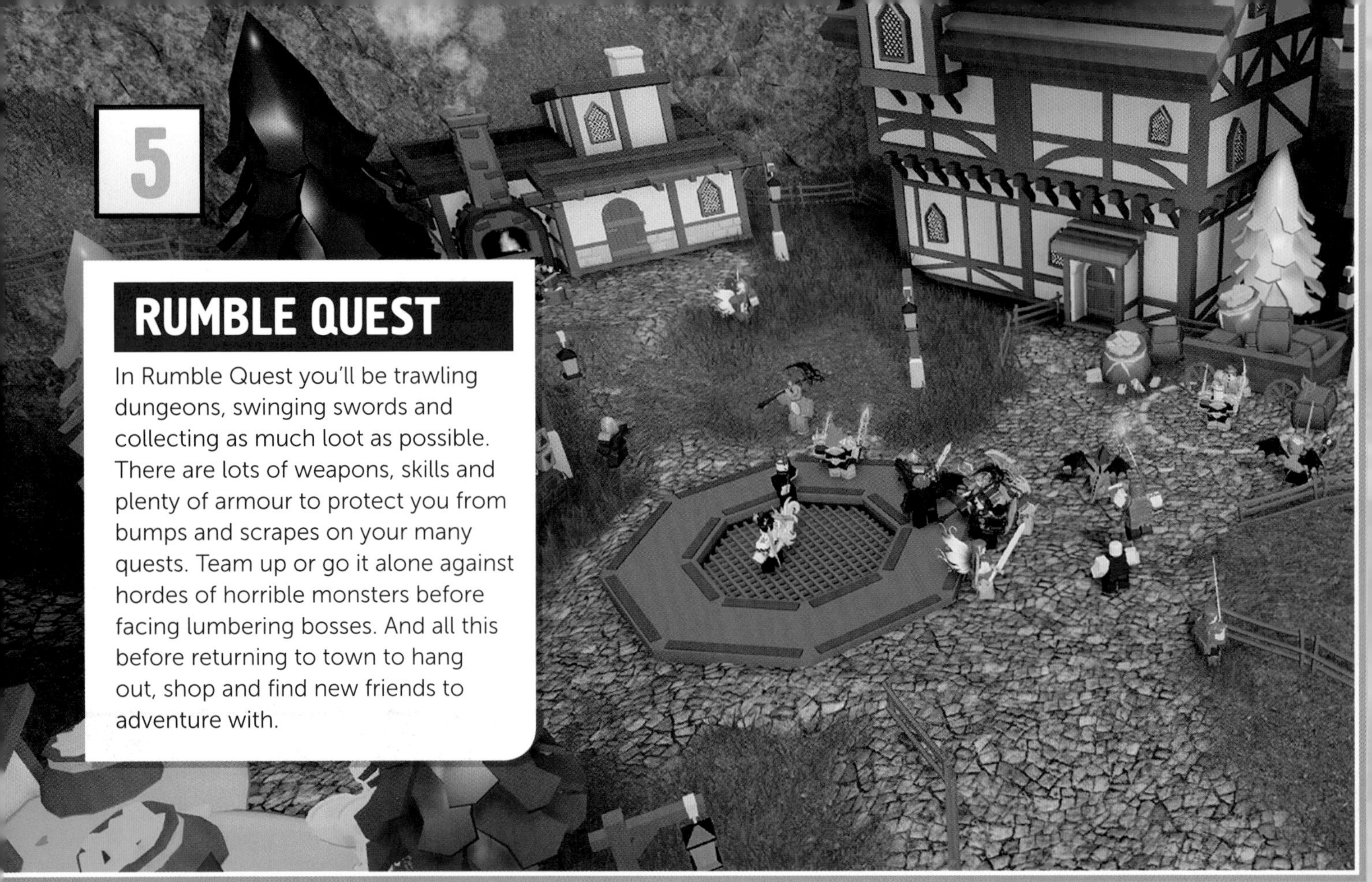

RUMBLE QUEST

In Rumble Quest you'll be trawling dungeons, swinging swords and collecting as much loot as possible. There are lots of weapons, skills and plenty of armour to protect you from bumps and scrapes on your many quests. Team up or go it alone against hordes of horrible monsters before facing lumbering bosses. And all this before returning to town to hang out, shop and find new friends to adventure with.

EMERGENCY RESPONSE

A role-playing game with a difference, Emergency Response features jobs simulating the best and bravest people, and those who oppose them. Choose from a handful of jobs, including firefighting and policing, or you can be the bad guy responsible for the chaos. Whether you're fighting fires or crime, each play session is different and lots of fun. Nothing beats tackling a blazing building and feeling pride when it's out.

BUILD AND SURVIVE!

If you and your friends are looking for a great co-op experience, Build and Survive! offers just that. Build bases and forts, collect items and weapons and work together in order to fight off swarms of monsters. With loads of different beasts and methods to eliminate them, you'll be trying to survive for hours. You can level up to unlock new skins and skills – try out the cannon ball blast, we think you'll love it!

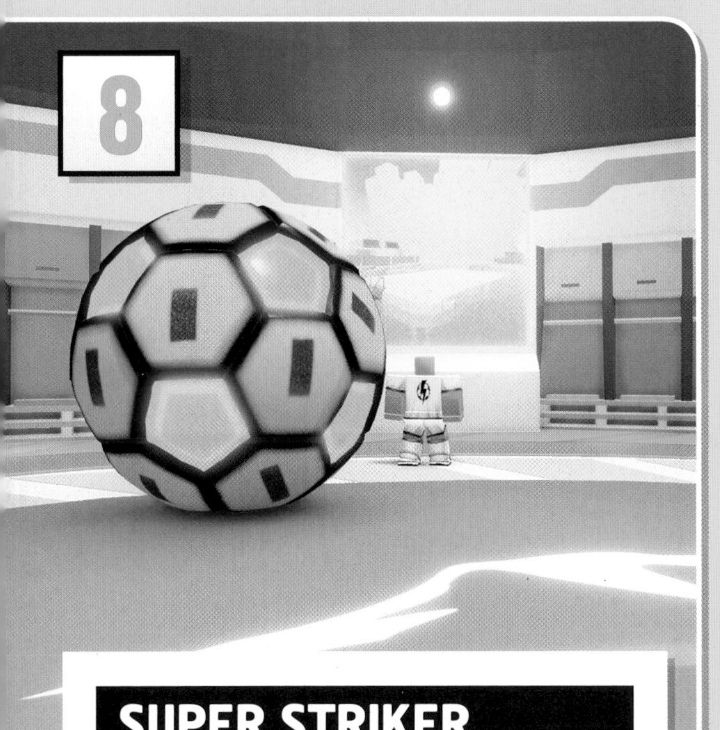

SUPER STRIKER LEAGUE

Easily the best football game on Roblox, the game is super-fun. It's not an overly serious sports sim though – the ball bounces around everywhere and scorelines regularly reach double figures. Of course, you can wear your silliest outfits on the pitch, so you can make it an even more beautiful game.

BOOGA BOOGA

An odd name for a survival game, but if just the name makes you smile then the rest of the game will bring you much enjoyment. By mining and gathering resources, you must survive the harsh world around you, governed by a hungry guide that you must offer sacrifices to. The game is always updated, bringing new enemies and items to play with and keep your adventure fresh.

10
Destruction Simulator can require a lot of power, so your machine may lag a little on the big bangs.

CONSTRUCTION SIMULATOR

Watching things break and shatter into tiny pieces is fun, but not safe. Or allowed. So, why not do it in Roblox? The game is simple: either head in on your own or with friends and destroy everything you can see. It's a physics-based game, so little pieces fly off everywhere, structures tumble to the ground and land with a crunch. It's very satisfying.

RTHRO

This recent addition to the Roblox universe gives players more control over what their avatar looks like. Rthro means more human-looking characters, rather than the original block-based style. This change isn't available in all games yet, but it's being rolled out to more every day.

You can see from this pair of avatars that the Rthro style really changes the basics of the models. Being stretched out, it gives a much more human look. The proportions are much less squat and blocky. Even though the changes are quite vast, all your old accessories and items will transfer easily to a new Rthro avatar.

You can easily see which games support Rthro styles by the small tag on the game image.

LEGENDS OF SPEED

In this speedy racing game, the object is to be the fastest player in the game. By completing races, levelling up your avatar and beating parkour challenges your avatar gets faster and faster until you're practically a blur! You'll need quick fingers to keep up with other players. When you aren't racing, there are plenty of mini-games to complete and pets to collect. Can you become the fastest Robloxian of all time?

THE FLOOR IS LAVA

Can you survive the rising lava? With over 100 maps to play, the lava is always a hazard. Using all your parkour and racing skills, you must complete each map to unlock awesome skills to help you survive. Of course, you want to look cool while avoiding a fiery ending and there are plenty of accessories to wear. Don't stop, just run!

MAGNET SIMULATOR

One of the most popular pet sims featuring the Rthro style, in Magnet Simulator your avatar can explore worlds, collect magnetic pets and seek out coins to expand your pet collection. There are plenty of challenges to attempt alongside your pet, or you can just hang out with friends to compare backpacks and clothes that you'll have won from contests. Magnet Simulator is attracting a huge crowd every day.

5 TYCOON GAMES

Tycoon games are big business on Roblox. Literally. The aim of nearly all of them is to make money; as much money as you can. Once you're rolling in cash, you can then make your tycoons even more productive.

1

THEME PARK TYCOON 2

The beauty of Theme Park Tycoon 2 is the ability to build exactly the rides you like in your fantasy park. You have to start off small, with a limited amount of money and rides, but as you please customers, your park rating goes up, unlocking more rides and attractions. Much like a real theme park, you have to be aware of your visitors' needs, keep it tidy, make sure they have food and drink and, of course, toilets!

2

VEHICLE TYCOON

Part tycoon game and part driving game, Vehicle Tycoon lets you build cars to sell to customers, or to drive around in order to earn more money. Buying better cars increases your reputation and there are a lot of cars! With lots of upgrades available for your car dealership, there's plenty to keep you busy.

3

SUPER HERO TYCOON

Making money here is all about the fighting. Once you've put together your ideal superhero, you'll need to fight the bad guys and keep everyone safe. Doing so will allow you to upgrade your base, unlocking more superpowers and different styles for your hero. You can happily build the heroes you already know and love, collecting weapons and other items to make things that bit more exciting.

4

LUMBER TYCOON 2

Chopping down trees makes a lot of money in this tycoon game. You can harvest wood, running it through your sawmill to make planks, then sell it off, which allows you to use the money to upgrade your factory. Lumber Tycoon 2 supports controller play on PC for those who prefer to avoid keyboard and mouse, and it features a ton of clever secrets for you to discover!

5

PIZZA FACTORY TYCOON

More pizza? You can never have enough of the stuff! Once you've chosen a nice plot of land, it's time to start making pizzas for visitors. There are lots of toppings to choose from and as you keep your customers happy, you'll be able to collect fun items throughout the land. Try to make the best, and worst, pizzas you can imagine.

TYCOON CLUES

Tycoons are all about making sure that your production line is working smoothly, so you need to make sure all parts are accounted for. Decipher the anagrams to find some important pieces in each tycoon game.

PIZZA TYCOON

1

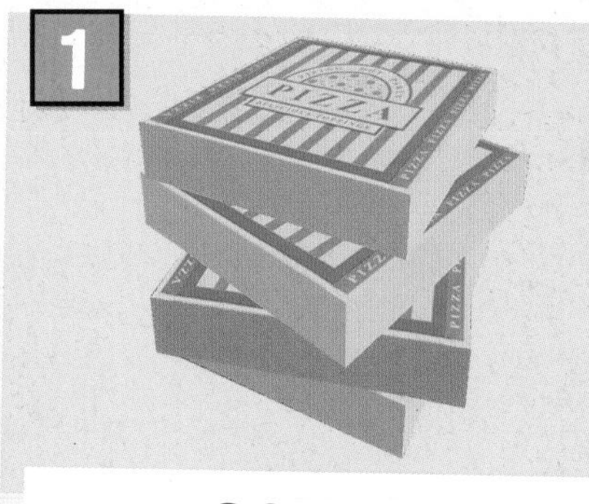

SOBEX

2

UHDOG

3

PIPTONGS

LUMBER TYCOON

1

RESET

2

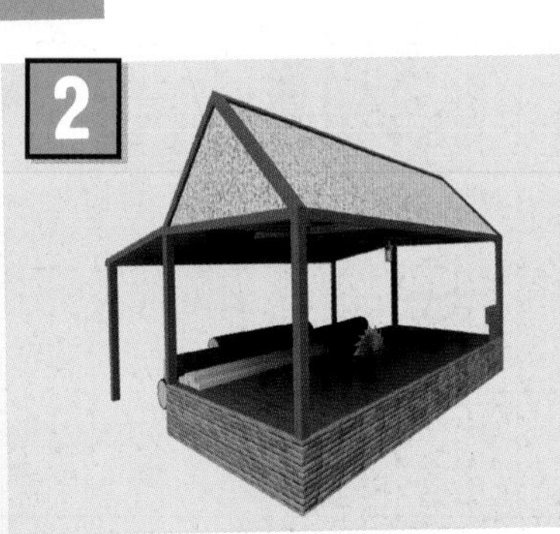

ALLSWIM

3

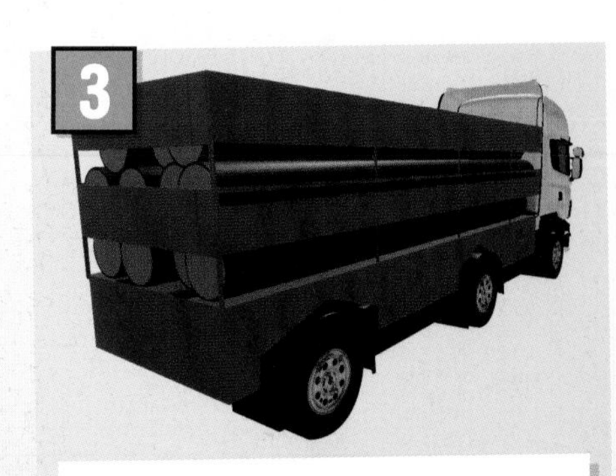

CARTUGROCK

If you're struggling to work out the answers, try visiting each game to see if you can get any more clues from playing!

Answers on page 69

THEME PARK TYCOON

1

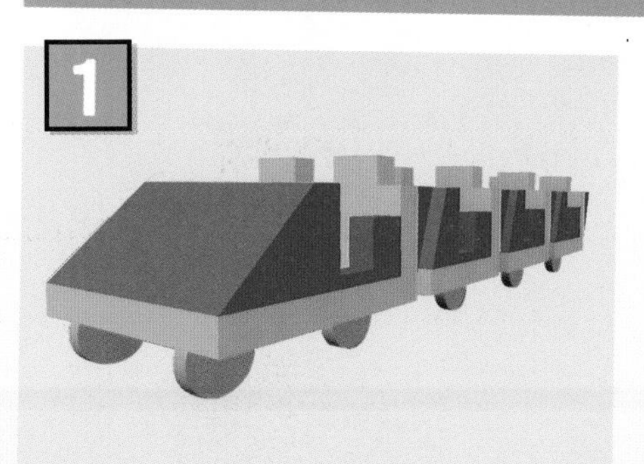

TERRORLOCALES

2

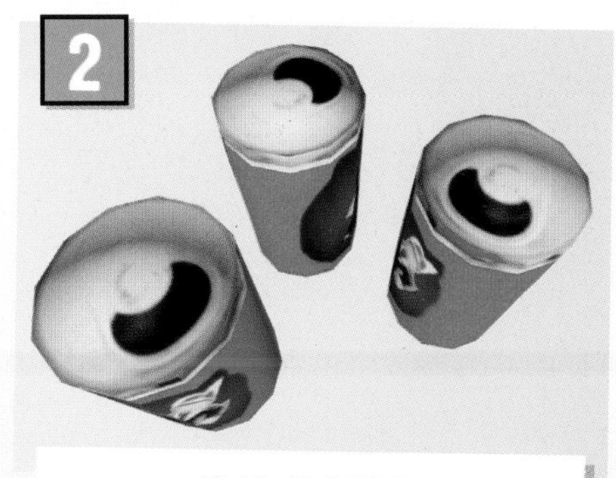

DRSINK

3

CUTPEAS

VEHICLE TYCOON

1

CHIELVES

2

OOHWORMS

3

MAYORTOW

SUPERHERO TYCOON

1

PUREPROWESS

2

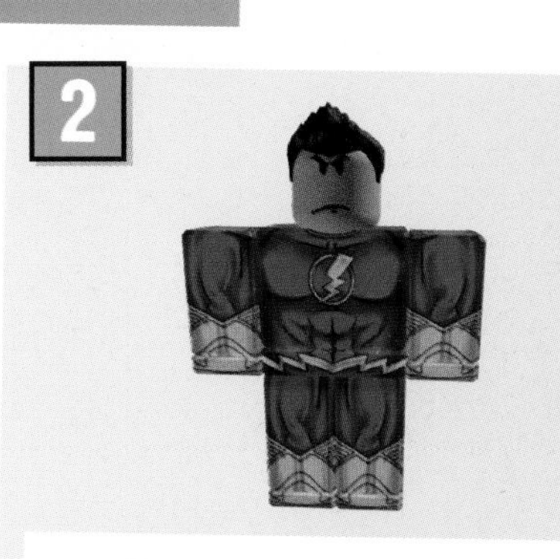

PERUSHORE

3

ILLVAIN

GAME CREATION

Game creation is a big part of Roblox. PC players will automatically have access to Roblox Studio, where you can bring your ideas to life and have thousands of players experience your vision. We've put together some tips and advice to help you create your very own Roblox game.

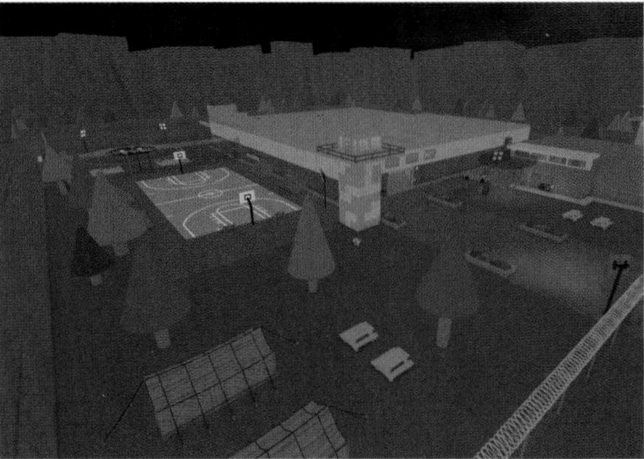

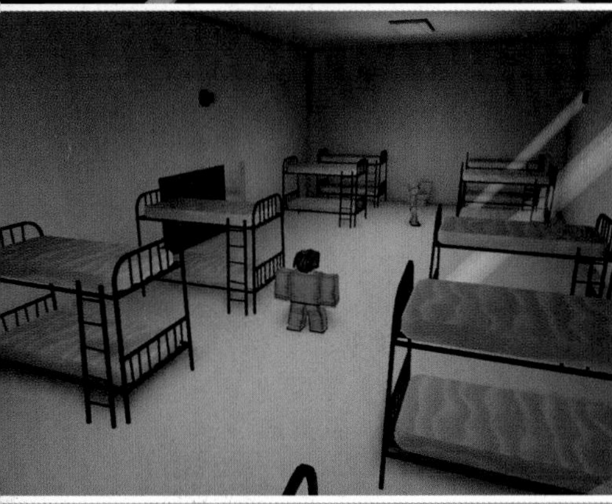

RESEARCH YOUR IDEA

So you have an idea for an amazing game – great! But before you even open up Roblox Studio, it's good to do some research. There are already so many games on the Roblox platform; explore the pages and see if your idea already exists. Don't be disheartened if there's something similar – play the game and see if you have something you can add to that style of game. Take inspiration from ideas that work and identify areas that you can improve on.

LEARN THE GENRE

You might be interested in turning your idea into a tycoon or obby, or something else entirely. All these genres have a fan base and that fan base might expect certain things from the genre. Play even more games in the genre and make a list of everything you find – if you notice something occurring in more than one game, like upgrades in a tycoon, it's likely that your intended audience will expect this. It's your choice whether to use the same things or not though.

BASIC DESIGN

Once you've got a sense of what you can add to a game, it's time to write down exactly what you will include. This will be the basic plan for your project. When you know that you need 10 different levels, for example, it's time to grab a pen and paper and start mapping out how each level will look. Don't worry about how to implement this in Studio just yet. You can start doodling map layouts, ideas for items or pets you'd like to include.

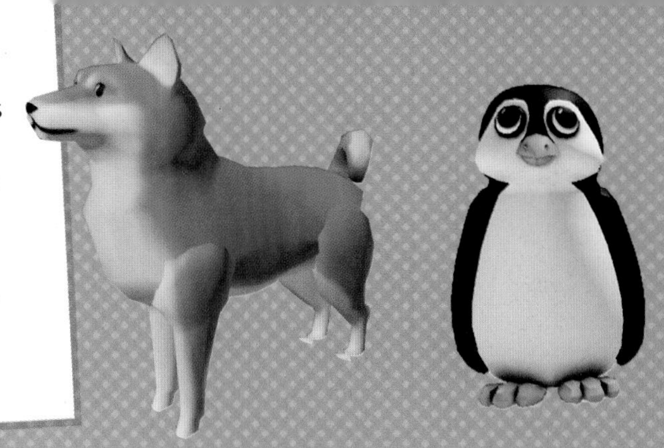

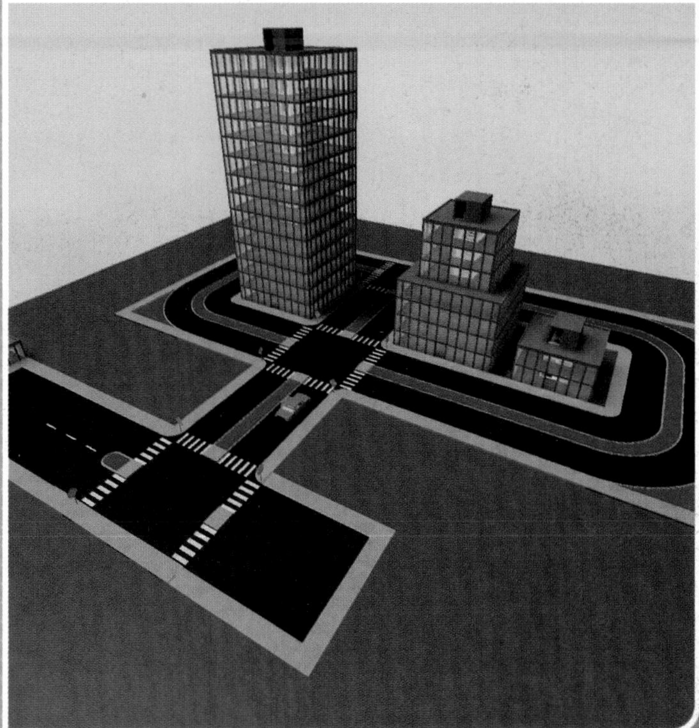

BROWSE THE STUDIO

Now it's time to open up the studio and have a good look around. Roblox Studio is designed to be simpler than other programming software. Don't be afraid to click on things to see what they do – you can always reset and start again. You can press 'Play' at any point to jump in and play your game. Try out one of the baseplates to play a fully-fledged game and see how you can change stuff around.

MAKE USE OF THE WEBSITE

The Roblox Studio website has everything you need in order to learn about game creation. Take a little time to read through the basics of building and coding in Studio. Understanding how to move the camera, change from creation to testing and how to save your progress are all functions you'll need to know first.

CHECK OUT TUTORIALS

The Internet has a ton of videos in which people make games on Roblox. Some of them are tutorials that you can follow step-by-step, while others show people building their own game. Some of the stuff you see might be daunting, but they're great for learning tips and tricks, no matter what stage your game is at.

START SMALL

It's very tempting to make your first game a big lifestyle game, full of pets and jobs. But that would mean learning a lot of new skills and possibly feeling overburdened with tools and items. Start with something small first. You might not start with the game you REALLY want to make, but you can make all the beginner mistakes on an idea that is more simple first of all. You'll also be able to get more familiar with the software and what is possible before moving on to bigger ideas.

CREATE WITH FRIENDS!

Game creation can be very difficult and almost every game you play on Roblox is made by a team of people rather than a solo developer. Why not try to bring your game idea to life with the help of your friends. For example, if you're comfortable with building in Studio, but not so good at coding, find a friend who is good at coding to work with. Sharing the workload will make it go much quicker! There are also lots of forums and message boards where you can ask for help if you need it.

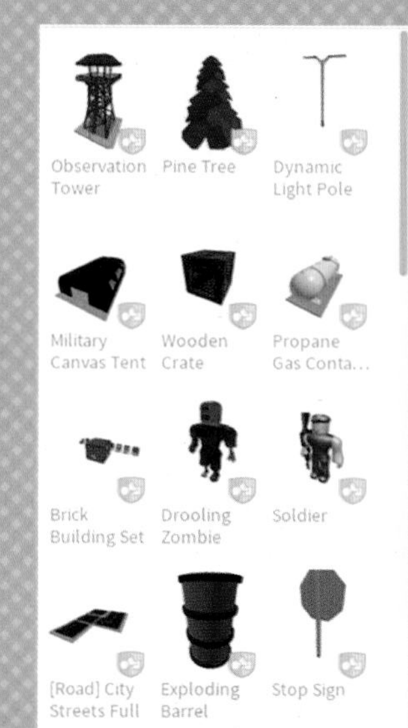

PLACEHOLDER ART

When you're familiar with Studio and have a good idea of how to build your game, you can start to create your game very roughly. You don't have to be particularly neat and tidy about what you're doing at the moment – you can just use simple shapes to build the map so that you have a template to iterate on. Studio also has a catalogue of items in the Toolbox that the community has built, which you can use for free!

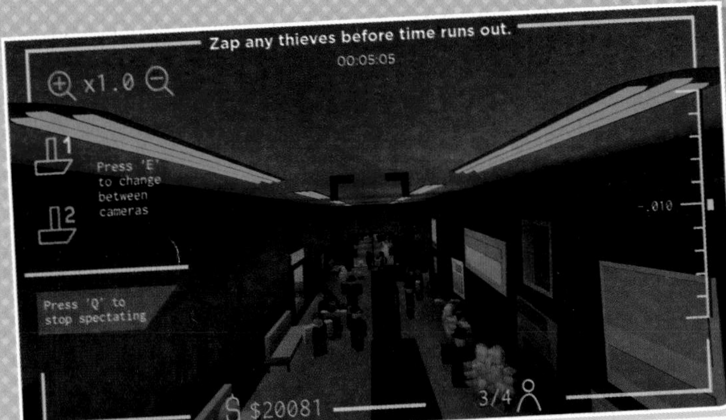

KEEP PLAYING

Make sure you play other games regularly too. It's easy to become so focused on your project that you forget to play other games, but playing games is just as valuable as reading tips and tricks. Maybe a new game comes out that has a really good map or a game mechanic that you haven't seen before. Or maybe it just has a better way of doing something that's in your game. Taking inspiration from other games isn't cheating!

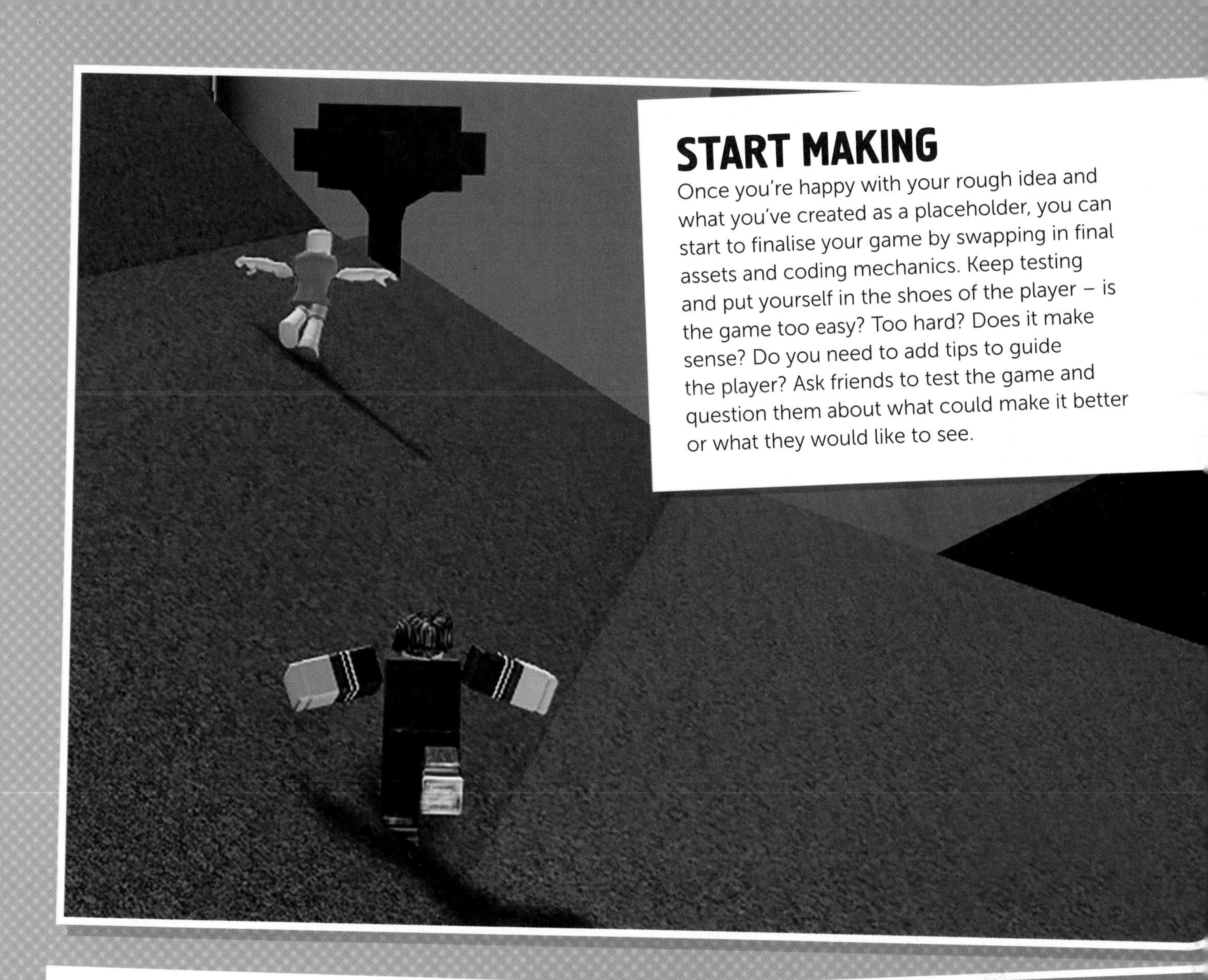

START MAKING

Once you're happy with your rough idea and what you've created as a placeholder, you can start to finalise your game by swapping in final assets and coding mechanics. Keep testing and put yourself in the shoes of the player – is the game too easy? Too hard? Does it make sense? Do you need to add tips to guide the player? Ask friends to test the game and question them about what could make it better or what they would like to see.

RELEASE IT!

It's time to release your game. You've worked on it for months. You've tested it, tried new things and you're confident it is finished. Get it onto the Roblox game pages and tell as many people as you can to play the game. However, the work doesn't stop here. Just because your game is in the world, that doesn't mean you're done. People WILL find bugs that will need updates, you'll want to support your game and if it's a success you'll probably want to add more content. Supporting your release is just as important as every other aspect of the creation process. Keep listening to players, find out what they want and help them as much as you can.

MORE

HIDDEN GEMS

It's time to find more nuggets of gaming joy from beyond the Roblox homepage. Here are five more games that you might not have heard of.

CUBE EAT CUBE

Using a familiar formula, Cube Eat Cube puts you in control of a cube who eats other cubes - the horror! With the aim of the game to become the biggest cube possible, you'll have to munch lots of smaller cubes. However, as you grow in size you get slower which makes you a target for those larger predators. A tap of a button splits you into smaller cubes for ease of movement, but the smaller you are, the easier you are to gulp down. A game that urges you to think tactically!

BEE SWARM SIMULATOR

Such a wonderfully cute game, where players must form a swarm of bees (one of the most important bugs on the planet) and use them to collect pollen, items and of course, honey. New bees hatch from eggs which can then harvest pollen in order to be turned into honey. Honey is then traded in for new eggs. It's a very simple game and we love it because of how peaceful it can be, just wandering around with your little bees, as part of nature.

GHOST SIMULATOR

We all know that the ghost's natural enemy is a vacuum cleaner. You didn't? Well, that's what you're given in Ghost Simulator. Pull those pesky ghosts into your vacuum to clear the different areas and use the ectoplasm to upgrade your kit or even adopt a pet. There are loads of characters to use, who all come with different challenges and skills. With so much to see and do, you can explore for ages and still have things to do. You're not afraid of ghosts, are you?

PROJECT LAZARUS

We love zombies! Or should that be, we hate zombies? We love zombie games ... that's better. And this one is great; full of tension and tactics. The idea is to survive a zombie apocalypse by using weapons and items to hold off swarms of the shambling dead. You need to work together to block off entryways and progress to harder rounds. No matter how good you are, there's always a way for a zombie to slip in and nom on your brains. At least here you can just start over again.

SCUBA DIVING AT QUILL LAKE

If you want more peaceful games, with less fast cars, weapons and explosions, then why not visit Quill Lake? Over 25 million people have dropped by and while they're here all they need to do is swim around and look for artefacts. These can then be sold in a nearby shop to upgrade your scuba equipment and find even more treasure. It's a lovely little underwater world which lets you escape the noisy real world for a while.

5 ADVENTURE GAMES

Adventure always means excitement, whether you're exploring a new world, tackling a difficult enemy or setting out on a dangerous mission. These games pit you as the hero in a variety of scenarios.

1

BUILD A BOAT FOR TREASURE

TREASURE! Is what we would shout if we ever found actual treasure. Instead we have to make do with either finding coins in the sofa or building a sweet boat in this game, as we have already seen. Once you've built your own boat, which can be as wacky or serious as you'd like, the hunt is on for that precious treasure. You can work as part of a team, but that would mean sharing the prize! Real pirates didn't share!

Did you know that the largest recorded treasure haul was dug up in 1840 and presented to Queen Victoria? It was worth approximately $3.2 million!

ARSENAL

If you want an all-action shooting game where the weapons are crazy, yet still feel great to use, then jump into Arsenal. There are great maps and some interesting items on show. Most intriguing is the golden knife, which you must use to actually win the game, but you can only acquire the weapon by using lower tier guns. It's like a reverse Battle Royale.

SHARKBITE

Which would you rather be, a sailor or a shark? A shark, right? Well, in this game you don't even have to choose. If you're a sailor, you will need a sturdy boat and weapons to fend off giant sharks. However, those who assume the role of shark will swim after friends, chomping on their boats and, quite possibly, their legs.

TREASURE HUNT SIMULATOR

Explore islands with treasures laying just below the ground. Dig that up, upgrade your kit – including a shovel, backpack and pets – then do it all over again! The deeper you go, the greater the treasure.

OP NINJA SIMULATOR

Yes! Ninjas! It's surely a fact that ninjas are the best and most dangerous fighters; creeping around dressed in black, throwing ninja stars and carrying beautiful swords. They harness magical powers to defeat their foes and in this ancient world based on Chinese fairytales, you can be a ninja like them. With lots of weapons and special powers, blast around the map taking out enemies and training to get better. We want to be ninjas!

DESIGN YOUR ULTIMATE HOME

Many of the games in Roblox allow you to design your dream home or ultimate fantasy room. Why not practise your designs here? It doesn't even need to be a house – maybe you want to design an awesome home cinema or a relaxing spa instead!

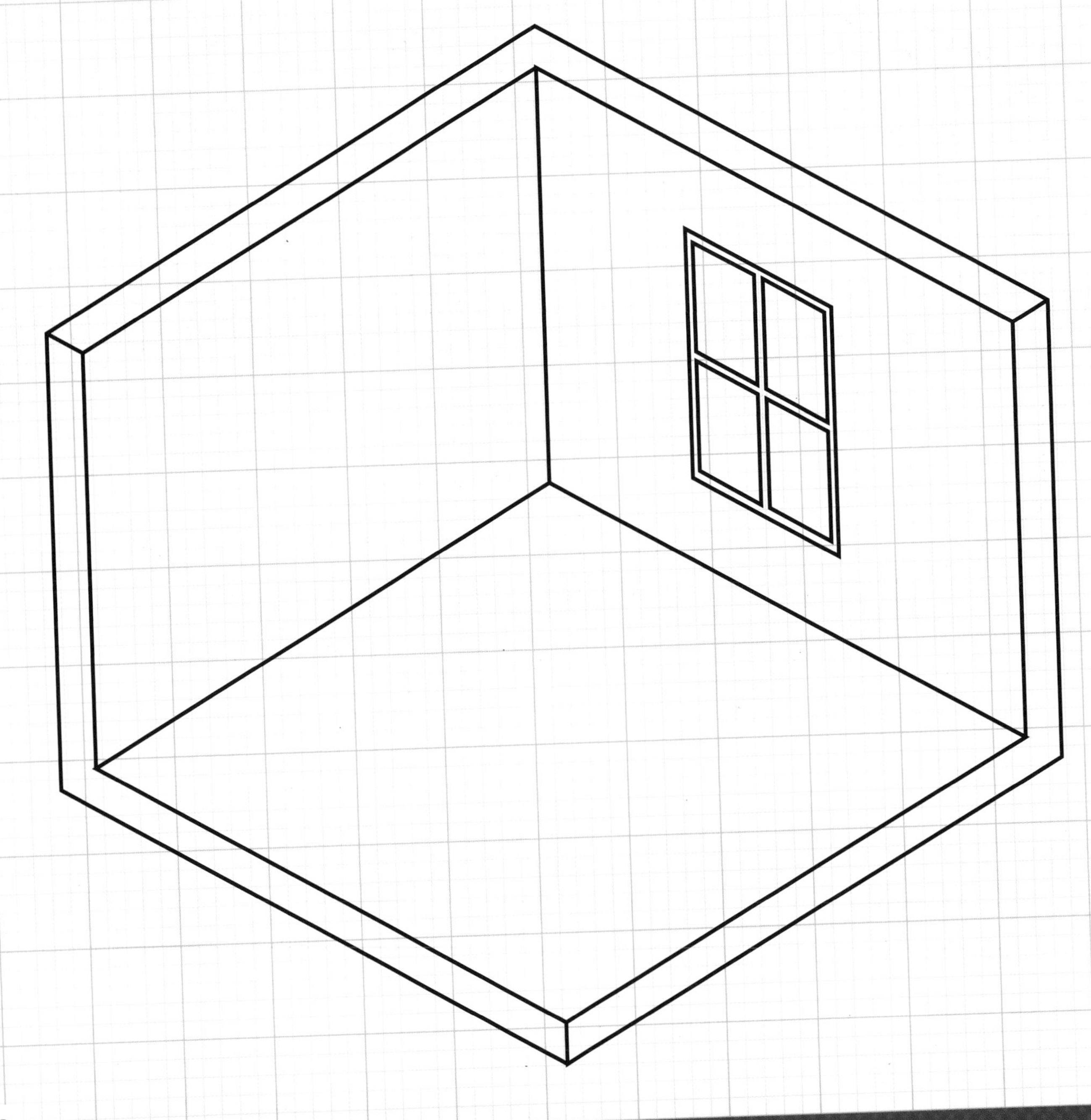

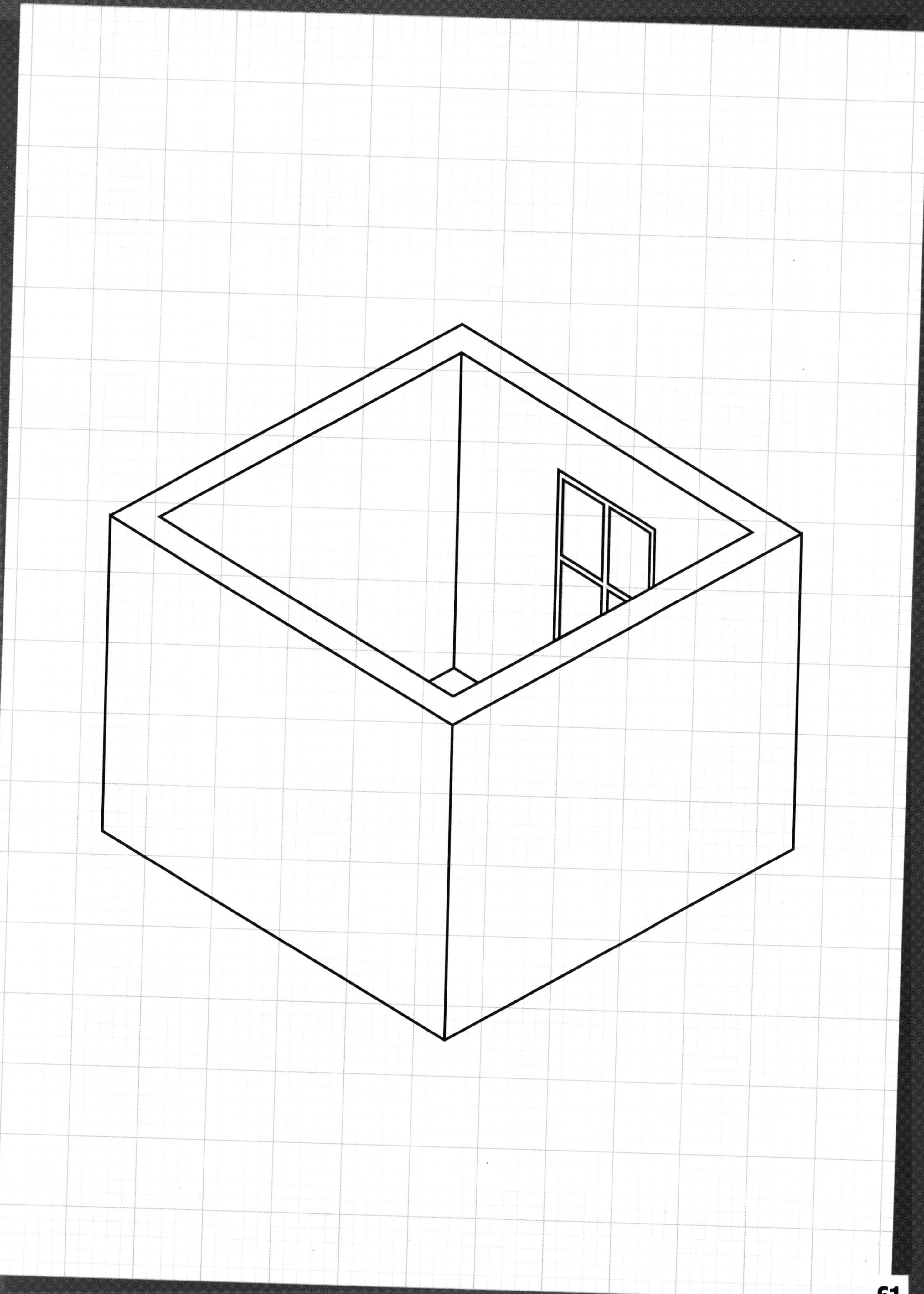

BEST PETS

So many of the games in Roblox feature adorable little pets who come in all shapes and sizes. Some are realistic, others are based on myth or even take the form of blobs of slime. They all have one thing in common... WE LOVE THEM!

MOUSE

ADOPT ME!

Starting small and simple, there's nothing like a pet that you can carry around with you. This little mouse is the perfect travel companion around Roblox.

MEEP

MEEPCITY

What is a Meep? Is it a cute living ball? Is it a legless octopus? Nobody really knows, but you'll see them everywhere you turn in MeepCity. That's right – they even named the whole city after these little guys.

SLIME

LAWN CUTTING SIMULATOR

Slime is funny, silly and, if you're lucky enough, it can be a wobbly friend to help you mow the grass! Available in many different colours and flavours.

SLIME

PET SIMULATOR 2

Of course, slimes come in many flavours. Those of Pet Simulator 2 are more laid-back and will simply bob along behind you.

DRAGON

ADOPT ME!

The Dragon is a rare pet in Adopt Me!, and once you have one, you'll be the envy of everyone else. Fortunately, we have no reports of any owners being scorched alive by their winged pets ... yet.

MORTUUS

PET SIMULATOR 2

A super strong pet found in Pet Simulator 2 is the Mortuus. It must be tough, it has four heads! Luckily each head has a sort-of friendly face. Sort of.

FINAL QUIZ

Can you find the correct answers to the questions below? Some of the answers should be on the previous pages.

Try playing the game in each question if you're struggling.

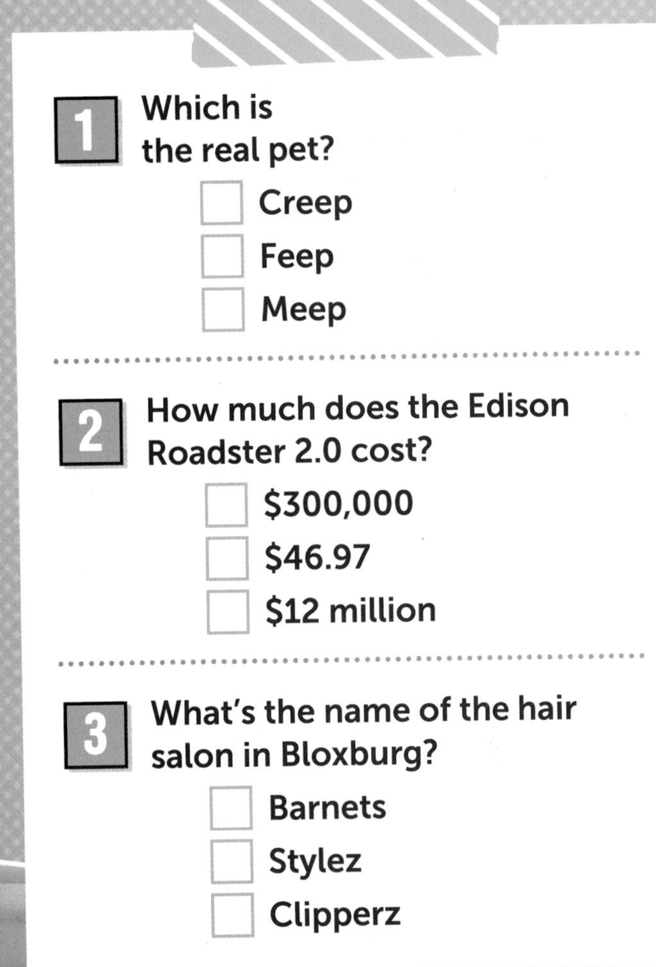

1 Which is the real pet?

- [ ] Creep
- [ ] Feep
- [ ] Meep

2 How much does the Edison Roadster 2.0 cost?

- [ ] $300,000
- [ ] $46.97
- [ ] $12 million

3 What's the name of the hair salon in Bloxburg?

- [ ] Barnets
- [ ] Stylez
- [ ] Clipperz

4 In Project Lazarus, what are you escaping from?

- [ ] Killer ponies
- [ ] Lions
- [ ] Zombies

5 What weapon do you use in Ghost Simulator?

- [ ] Sword
- [ ] Vacuum
- [ ] Magic Wand

6 What does 'Obby' mean?

- [ ] Obstacle
- [ ] Obvious
- [ ] Oblivion

7 What is the name of the new style of avatar?

- [ ] Anthro
- [ ] Arthur
- [ ] Rthro

8 How many heads does the Mortuus have?

- [ ] 8
- [ ] 4
- [ ] 1

9 Which playground game is 'extreme'?

- [ ] Hide and Seek
- [ ] Tag
- [ ] Football

10 What colour is the winning knife in Arsenal?

- [ ] Gold
- [ ] Blue
- [ ] Red

11 What food do you need to harvest in Bee Simulator?

- [ ] Hot dogs
- [ ] Bread
- [ ] Honey

12 Which genre is all about earning money and upgrading?

- [ ] Manager
- [ ] Shopping
- [ ] Tycoon

13 What vehicle do we build to find treasure?

- [ ] Boat
- [ ] Racing car
- [ ] Plane

14 Who catches the criminals in Jailbreak?

- [ ] Baker
- [ ] Police
- [ ] Vet

Answers on page 69

GOODBYE

We've been on quite a journey across these pages, haven't we?

We visited MeepCity and Bloxburg, collected lots of pets and worked many jobs. We raced cars, opened Pizza restaurants and decorated houses. Above all, we had fun. It's clear that Roblox offers so many possibilities when it comes to playing games.

We took time to learn how to make our own games that we can show off to our friends. We dressed up, unlocked skills and accessories and we discovered lots of new games to play.

There's a whole world out there to explore, either on your own or with your friends. Why not try out some new games or gather your friends and discover new ways to play together?

Remember to stay safe online, ask permission where you need to and always play nicely. Goodbye from us ... until next time!

STAYING SAFE ONLINE

YOUNGER FANS' GUIDE

Spending time online is great fun. These games might be your first experience of digital socialising, here are a few simple rules to help you stay safe and keep the internet an awesome place to spend time:

- Never give out your real name – don't use it as your username.
- Never give out any of your personal details.
- Never tell anybody which school you go to or how old you are.
- Never tell anybody your password, except a parent or guardian.
- Before registering for any account, ask a parent or guardian for permission.
- Take regular breaks, as well as playing with parents nearby, or in shared family rooms.
- Always tell a parent or guardian if something is worrying you.

PARENTS' GUIDE

ONLINE CHAT

In most games, there is live on-screen text chat between users. Parents are advised to ensure that their children are only talking to friends and that they aren't being exposed to any adult matter.

SOUND

Sound is crucial in many video games. Players will often wear headphones, meaning parents won't be able to hear what children are listening to. Set up your console or computer to have sound coming from the TV or monitor as well as the headset so you can hear what your child is experiencing.

REPORTING PLAYERS

If you see or hear a player being abusive, Roblox allows you to report users or interactions. You'll be able to use the Report Abuse links found throughout the site on game pages, but there may also be buttons within chat windows or game menus where you can raise a case with community managers.

SCREEN TIME

Taking regular breaks is important. Set play sessions by using a timer. Some games can last a long time and if your child finishes playing in the middle of a round, they could leave their teammates a person short and lose any points they've earned. It is advisable to give an advanced warning for stopping play or clearly outlining a stopping point before play begins.

IN-GAME PURCHASES

Many games offer in-app purchases to enhance the game experience but they're not required to play the game. They also don't improve a player's performance. There are ways to set up safety measures on you child's account by setting up a PIN through Settings. Consult these before allowing your child to play any game in order to avoid any unpermitted spending on your account.

ANSWERS

Page 20 - Career Quiz

Baker, Miner, Teacher, Waiter, Artist, Shopkeeper, Racer, Doctor, Banker

Page 24 - Spot the Difference

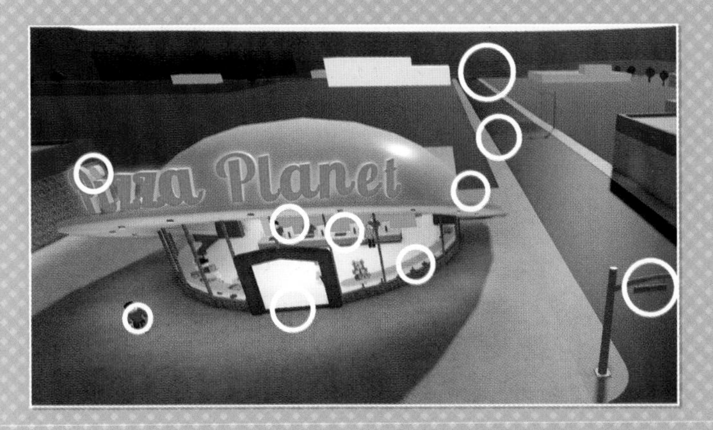

Page 25 - Hidden Objects

Page 30 - Maze Race

Page 38 - Car Sudoku

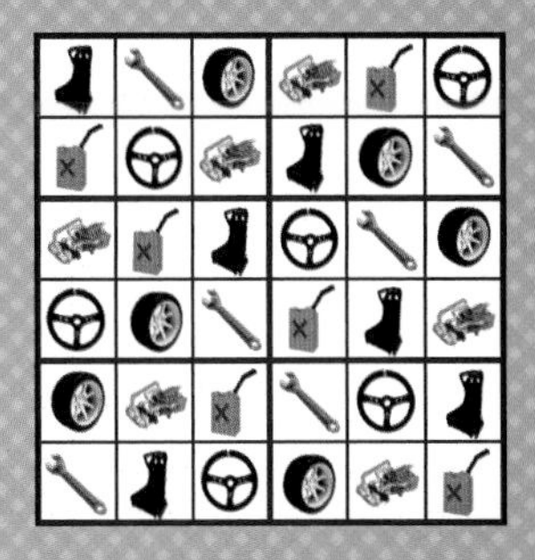

Page 39 - Speed Maze

Page 48 - Tycoon Clues

Pizza Tycoon:
1. Boxes, 2. Dough, 3. Toppings

Lumber Tycoon:
1. Trees, 2. Sawmill, 3. Cargo Truck

Theme Park Tycoon:
1. Rollercoaster, 2. Drinks, 3. Teacups

Vehicle Tycoon:
1. Vehicle, 2. Showroom, 3. Motorway

Superhero Tycoon:
1. Superpowers, 2. Superhero, 3. Villain

Page 64 - Final Quiz

1. Meep, 2. $12 million, 3. Stylez, 4. Zombies, 5. Vacuum, 6. Obstacle, 7. Rthro, 8. 4, 9. Hide and Seek, 10. Gold, 11. Honey, 12. Tycoon, 13. Boat, 14. Police.